How to Design a Vocational Curriculum

How to Design a Vocational Curriculum

A Practical
Guide for
Schools
and
Colleges

Tony Nasta

KOGAN
PAGE

London • Philadelphia

First published in 1994

Kogan Page Limited
120 Pentonville Road
London N1 9JN

British Library Cataloguing in Publication Data

A CIP record for this book is available from the British Library

ISBN 0 7494 1112 0

Typeset by BookEns Ltd., Baldock, Herts.
Printed and bound in Great Britain by Biddles Ltd,
Guildford and King's Lynn.

Contents

5

CONTENTS

Acknowledgements

I should like to express my thanks to my former colleagues at the Suffolk College who have supported me in the production of this book.

This book would not have been completed at all without the support of my wife, Jan Cullum Nasta, and I am indebted to her for her encouragement and help.

Introduction

This book is intended for staff in schools and colleges grappling with the complex problem of designing and implementing a vocational curriculum. It will also be of great use to students preparing for a career which involves teaching the post-14 age group.

The vocational curriculum is currently under scrutiny and of close interest to government, employers and educationalists. All have drawn attention to the vital importance of increasing participation rates in post-compulsory education in the UK. The learning needs of neither full-time students staying on beyond 16 nor the increasing number of adult students are likely to be satisfied through the academic route alone.

The eight chapters in this book have been written to provide practical help to curriculum designers in schools and colleges, currently developing vocational courses. There is detailed explanation and evaluation of important processes including: the preparation of submissions for validation, the designing of flexible learning programmes, the assessment of competence and core skills, the implementation of credit accumulation and transfer, the accreditation of prior learning, the development of franchising and quality control.

Each chapter has been written to stand on its own; therefore the reader who is primarily interested in assessment or the accreditation of prior learning (APL), for instance, can turn immediately to the relevant page. The chapters follow a broadly similar approach, which includes an explanation of the context of the issue, an evaluation of the implications for curriculum design and some illustrative examples, where appropriate.

All curriculum designers are aware of the important implications of the development of NVQs and GNVQs for vocational education. As well as providing practical guidance on how to design and assess outcome-based programmes, this book also relates NVQs and GNVQs to the broader educational principles which inform good practice.

1 A Changing Vocational Curriculum

The vocational curriculum is a changing curriculum. The government has set ambitious growth targets in order to increase the participation rates of both 16- to 18-year olds and adult learners, as the system moves to one of mass vocational education. The rapid development of National and General National Vocational Qualifications (NVQs and GNVQs) represents an attempt to bring coherence into an area characterised by a huge diversity of qualifications. Alongside these changes, there has been a fundamental re-organisation of the institutions – schools, colleges and universities – which offer vocational qualifications. The system of local authority control has given way to a new model of more autonomous institutions which are funded by central bodies. These changes set the context for the central concern of this book: how to design a vocational curriculum. The purpose of this chapter is to briefly describe both the legacy, and some of the current directions of change, before turning to the critical design features of a vocational curriculum. Four themes form the basis of the discussion: diversity, growth, coherence and change.

The legacy – a diverse system

There is no single vocational curriculum, but a range of different curricula which have developed in an incremental way over time. There are over 150 examining and awarding bodies and over 1,700 qualifications. Historically, there has been no national body to control the setting up of examining and awarding bodies in England. As new professions and crafts have developed, new training and qualification routes have been created in a piecemeal fashion.There is consequently a wide range of organisations able to offer qualifications in the vocational education sector. The development of the different bodies reflects distinct traditions in craft and apprenticeship training, in academic and general vocational education and in professional recruitment and development. Despite the setting up of the National Council for Vocational Qualifications (NCVQ) in 1986 with the purpose of rationalising all vocational qualifications, the diversity of qualifications remains a critical feature of the sector.

The classification below, based upon the UDACE/FEU publication, *Understanding Accreditation* (Ecclestone, 1992), provides a simple guide to the main organisations responsible for offering qualifications in vocational education. (Note: UDACE stands for the Unit for the Development of Adult Continuing Education which in 1992 was merged into the Further Education Unit − FEU.)

National awarding bodies

These are involved in the accreditation of a wide range of national vocational provision, including qualifications accredited as NVQs and GNVQs. Between them, the national awarding bodies account for some 80 per cent of vocational qualifications. Each awarding body has its own distinct arrangements for the assessment, control and certification of its awards. The major bodies include:

- Business and Technology Education Council (BTEC)
- City and Guilds of London Institute (C&G)
- Royal Society of Arts Examinations Board (RSA)
- Pitman Examination Institute.

Professional associations

A large number of professional bodies offer their own accreditation and increasingly validate colleges to run courses and programmes across further, higher and adult education. The professional bodies have developed historically to represent their members and to protect the standards of training. They offer a wide range of qualifications, often studied through part-time courses in general further education colleges. Examples of professional bodies include:

- Nursery Nursing Examining Board
- Institute of Meat
- Chartered Insurance Institute
- Council for Licensed Conveyancers.

Some professional body qualifications have been accredited as NVQs. Accreditation for programmes leading to professional body awards is sometimes carried out in conjunction with the national awarding bodies such as BTEC.

Membership bodies

Some membership bodies also validate courses and learning programmes:

- trade unions
- chambers of commerce

Open College Networks

OCNs are locally based and controlled networks which operate within a national framework provided through the National Open College Network (NOCN). They offer accreditation for locally designed programmes based in the workplace, the community, voluntary organisations or colleges. OCNs award credits and certificates for achievements on recognised programmes. These are usually designed to recognise the achievements of adult learners and to consequently provide them with a qualification which allows progression into further or higher education.

The variety of accreditation and awarding arrangements has led many commentators to describe the system as a qualifications jungle. It is probable that the complexity of the sector has denied access to many students because they simply do not understand the system. The attempt to develop greater coherence, through the rapid introduction of National Vocational Qualifications, is designed to lead to a much greater take-up of vocational qualifications.

The system is also diverse in the sense that there is a range of different organisations offering the above qualifications. These include secondary schools, general further education colleges, sixth form colleges, tertiary colleges, universities and specialist colleges, such as art and agricultural colleges. Vocational qualifications are thus available at a number of levels spanning secondary, further and higher education. The main focus of this book is upon the nature of the design process of the vocational curriculum, which has a number of common features in whatever institutional context it is delivered.

The future – growth and greater participation?

The emphasis upon growth has come from many sources. Industrial and business interests have seen the expansion and modernisation of the system of vocational training as an essential prerequisite for the regeneration of a flagging industrial economy. A number of educationalists have also stressed the central importance of lifelong education and training in a society in which occupations are increasingly dependent upon the capacity to rapidly assimilate and communicate complex knowledge and information. As a result of such pressures, the government has committed itself to ambitious plans for the expansion of further and higher education. This commitment to expansion has been embodied in the targets set for institutions by the further and higher education funding councils.

The National Education and Training Targets (NETTS) reproduced in Figure 1.1 are illustrative of this commitment to growth. The NETTS are being strongly promoted by the Training and Enterprise Councils (TECs) as a strategy for raising the occupational skill levels of the British workforce. They are also supported by a wide range of industrial interests such as the Confederation of British Industry, the Institute of Directors and a number of the largest trade unions. The Further Education Funding Council (FEFC) also makes reference to the NETTS in its stated aims.

Foundation targets
1. By 1997, 80 per cent of young people to reach NVQ2 or equivalent.
2. Training and education to NVQ3 or equivalent to be available to all young people who can benefit.
3. By 2000, 50 per cent of young people to reach NVQ3 or equivalent.
4. Education and training provision to develop self-reliance, flexibility and breadth.

Lifetime learning
1. By 1996, all employees should take part in training or development activities.
2. By 1996, 50 per cent of the work force to be aiming for NVQs or units towards them.
3. By 2000, 50 per cent of the work force to be qualified to at least NVQ3 or equivalent.
4. By 1996, 50 per cent of medium to larger organisations (200 or more employees) to be 'Investors in People.'

Figure 1.1 *The National Education and Training Targets (NETTS)*

It is interesting to note the commitment to lifetime learning expressed by the NETT targets. This is a commitment which is echoed in a number of influential reports by leading educationalists. In the 1991 RSA report, *Learning Pays*, Christopher Ball writes:

> the RSA's vision ... is for a learning society in the UK. A learning society would be one in which everyone participated in education and training throughout their life. It would support them as citizens in their employment and their leisure. A learning society would also make provision to match these enhanced aspirations. The translation of aspirations into reality cannot be achieved by government alone. It requires the co-operation, effort and enterprise of many agencies and all parts of society (Ball, 1991, p.6).

In a similar vein Sir Claus Moser, introducing the 1993 *National Education Commission* proposals for an increase in national spending on education, stated:

> education is the one form of spending which links with everything else, such as the state of the economy. The bill is not outrageous when you view it in the long term (Moser, 1993).

Promoting a more coherent system

The diverse range of vocational qualifications has arguably been a major factor in inhibiting access for learners. The existence of a vast number of awarding bodies each promoting the unique value of their own qualifications has created a sense of confusion. Historically, the UK has lacked a national system of vocational qualifications. Given the fragmentation of the vocational alternatives, it is not surprising that there has been an exaggerated stress on the academic route represented by the study of GCE A levels, followed by a degree. The British tradition of providing a rigorous academic education for a small proportion of the population through the established universities has also led to an undervaluing of the vocational routes.

The NCVQ was set up in 1986 with the remit of establishing a national system of vocational qualifications (NVQs) to cover all occupations. It is responsible for accrediting qualifications submitted by the awarding bodies which must conform to the standards specified by industry lead bodies. The nature of the NCVQ accreditation process and the role played by lead bodies is outlined in Figure 1.2. This diagram illustrates that NCVQ has not been created as an awarding body. Its prime function is to create a national framework to which the awards offered by the national awarding bodies and professional associations must conform. It exercises control over the system of vocational qualifications by first defining the occupational standards, through its lead bodies, and then through its power of giving or withholding accreditation to the awards offered by the national awarding bodies such as BTEC and City and Guilds.

In order to gain NVQ accreditation for a specific qualification,

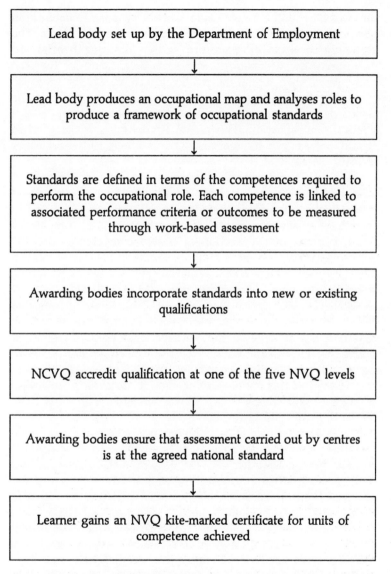

Source: This diagram is based upon an illustration which first appeared in Ecclestone, 1992.

Figure 1.2 *The NCVQ accreditation process*

the awarding body must ensure that its proposed qualification conforms to the standards established by the lead body. The awarding body will therefore design its qualification to incorporate the occupational standards determined by the lead body. It will then submit its qualification to NCVQ for approval. If successful in gaining approval, it will agree to monitor the standards of assessment of any college or other centre which offers the qualification. This external monitoring is designed to ensure that centres, colleges and schools adhere to the principles of NVQ assessment.

National Vocational Qualifications are thus statements of work-related outcomes to which the learning programmes offered by colleges or other providers must conform. An NVQ accredited qualification is broken down into units of competence which consists of a collection of related competences and the performance criteria governing assessment. There is also a description of the context or environment, known as the range statement, in which the competence will be displayed.

As the NCVQ system has evolved, it has become clear that NVQs are primarily designed for people in employment seeking to broaden and develop their occupational skills. There is no doubt that NCVQ has sought to create much greater access to vocational training and assessment, for those at work, through the creation of this national framework. It has made a great deal of progress in defining occupational standards at the first three levels, the craft and technician levels.

NVQs are available at five different levels covering a range of specialist occupational areas. The growth in the number of separate NVQs, together with the growth in the number of lead bodies, has led many to question whether or not NCVQ has achieved the rationalisation of vocational qualifications intended in its initial mission. Indeed history may prove that the more recent introduction of the General National Vocational Qualifications (GNVQ) may have far more impact in creating a more coherent vocational route, at least for full-time students.

The GNVQ is a qualification primarily for full-time students in schools and colleges, which was first announced in the 1991 White Paper, *Education and Training for the 21st Century* (DES, 1991). Its objective is to provide a recognised vocational alternative to GCE A levels – hence the colloquial description, 'vocational A levels' which is increasingly being used to describe GNVQ. NCVQ plays a similar role in the accreditation of GNVQ as with NVQs. Three national awarding bodies have been accredited to offer GNVQs: BTEC, City and Guilds and RSA. GNVQs are offered at three levels. Advanced GNVQ or Level 3 is equivalent to GCE A level. Intermediate GNVQ or Level 2 is designed to be of a comparable standard to 4 GCSEs at grade C or above. Foundation GNVQ or Level 1 overlap with the National Curriculum at keystage 4 and may be taken with a number of GCSE subjects.

The significance of GNVQs is that the three major vocational awarding bodies, which between them account for 80 per cent of the vocational qualifications awarded in England and Wales, will offer a qualification with a common structure, a common assessment framework and a common definition of the three levels. This degree of compatibility between the qualifications within the vocational route is unprecedented and does offer the opportunity, at last, of building a genuine national vocational alternative to the academic route for full-time students. Since the piloting of GNVQ qualifications in 1992 there has been immense interest in the new qualification and a rapid take-up in many secondary schools and colleges.

The position of BTEC, RSA and City and Guilds will be comparable to that of the GCE A level examining boards, in that they will all be offering a very similar nationally approved vocational qualification in competition with each other. As GNVQ qualifications replace the current vocational awards, such as the City and Guilds Diploma in Vocational Education and the BTEC National Diploma, a nationally recognised vocational qualification will gradually have become established. The timetable for the phasing in of GNVQ qualifications in different occupational areas is shown in Figure 1.3.

GNVQs share a number of characteristics with NVQ qualifications. Each GNVQ qualification is made up of a number of individual units. Each unit is specified in the form of the learning outcomes to be achieved. Credit can be gained for individual units, whether or not the student completes the whole qualification. The credit accumulation framework allows students the opportunity of building up credit towards a GNVQ over time. It also allows GNVQ units to be combined with other qualifications, such as GCE A levels or GCSEs. It is this flexibility which is the prime attraction of GNVQ qualifications. The approach to the assessment of GNVQ qualifications is also similar to NVQs: it is based upon the student producing evidence to demonstrate the achievement of performance criteria.

All GNVQ qualifications consist of three types of units: core skill units, such as communication, application of number and information technology, which are common to all GNVQ qualifications at the same level; mandatory units, which are common to a defined vocational area such as science or art and design; finally, there are optional units which are designed by the three awarding bodies in accordance with criteria set for GNVQs, by the NCVQ. The detailed description of the structure, learning styles and assessment arrangements of these new vocational qualifications is taken up in the chapters which follow.

	1992–3	1993–4	1994–5	1995–6
Art and Design	Pilot			
Business	Pilot			
Health and Social Care	Pilot			
Leisure and Tourism	Pilot			
Manufacturing	Pilot			
Built Environment		Pilot		
Hospitality and Catering		Pilot		
Science		Pilot		
Distribution			Pilot	
Engineering			Pilot	
Information Technology			Pilot	
Land-based Industries			Pilot	
Management			Pilot	
Media and Communication			Pilot	

Source: GNVQ Information Note, September 1993

Figure 1.3 *Timetable for introduction of intermediate and advanced GNVQs*

The development of NVQs and GNVQs alongside the established GCSE and GCE A level routes will eventually lead to three main post-compulsory qualification routes as illustrated by Figure 1.4. The GCE A level route will remain, for the time being at least, as an academic route to higher education in the form of undergraduate and postgraduate study. The NVQ route, with its five levels, is becoming established as the main qualification route for those in employment seeking further education and training. The GNVQ route draws upon both the academic and employment-based routes to provide a broad general education and preparation for the world of work or higher education. These three routes are not all fully in place, but it is clearly the intention of the government and NCVQ that future coherence will be based upon this pattern of provision.

Managing change – the challenge of curriculum design

The 1990s have been a turbulent period for the curriculum designer in vocational education, with one change after another impacting upon the curriculum. Perhaps, one theme above all others is most critical and this is the replacement of vocational courses by learning programmes.

The notion of a course reflects the traditional world of vocational education. A course is an integrated curriculum designed by professional educationalists, usually at a national level, by awarding or professional bodies. The course is usually delivered over a standard academic year by schools and colleges. Most elements of the course are compulsory for students – the whole is seen as more than the sum of the parts. It is therefore unusual for the student to gain exemption from part or all of the course because of prior knowledge or experience. The pedagogical model of the curriculum is paramount, namely that there is a recognised and authoritative body of knowledge which has to be imparted by teachers to learners in a prescribed format, in a prescribed order and over a prescribed period of time.

The notion of a learning programme challenges all these

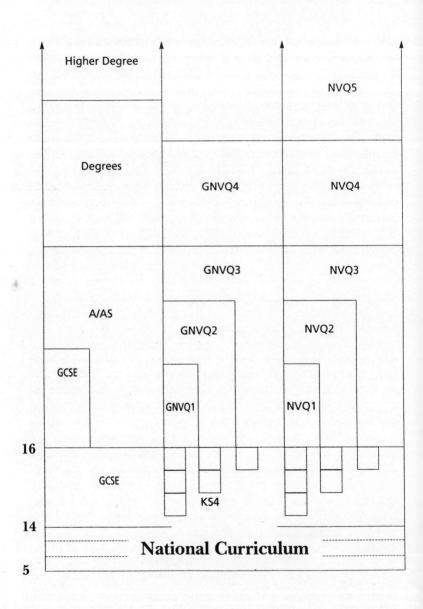

Figure 1.4 *National qualification framework*

conventions. Entry and exit points for learners depend upon achievements both prior to and during the period of study. There are no in-built assumptions about the speed at which individuals can learn in order to gain credit towards a qualification. The delivery of learning programmes is not therefore constrained by the conventional academic year. Programmes are constructed using the building blocks of units or modules which represent discrete units of assessment. The whole qualification becomes the sum of the parts, in a form which is quite unlike the conventional course. In the learning programme, the cohesion and integration of knowledge and skills become a function of the learner's desire and ability to make connections between the different modules. The concept of the learning programme thus challenges the pedagogical model of the curriculum, which is based on the belief that educationalists need to design integrated courses to lead the learner progressively to an holistic perspective. In the learning programme, the student exercises choice, creates integration and negotiates learning outcomes. Learning becomes a partnership between the teacher as facilitator and the student as client.

This critical distinction between courses and learning programmes underpins much of the discussion in this book. It is quite clearly related to the implementation of NVQs and GNVQs which are designed as learning programmes. The subsequent chapters deal with the design features of both courses and learning programmes. This is in recognition of the fact that courses will continue to co-exist with learning programmes for many years and that many of the awarding bodies will continue to stress the virtues of a course-based curriculum.

Summary

This chapter has attempted to highlight some of the major features of change in the vocational curriculum. Four themes have formed the basis of the discussion: diversity, growth, coherence and change. This brief discussion forms the backcloth for the analysis of different aspects of the process of designing a vocational curriculum such as student centred learning, assessment and validation. These separate strands form the components of the rest of this book.

Further reading and references

Ball, C (1991) *Learning Pays: the role of post-compulsory education and training:* London: RSA.

DES (1991) *Education and Training for the 21st Century*, Vol 1, London: HMSO.

Ecclestone, K (1992) *Understanding Accreditation: ways of recognising achievement*, London: Unit for the Development of Adult Continuing Education.

Moser, Sir Claus (1993) quoted in the *Independent* 16 November 1993.

Nasta, T (1993) *Change through Networking in Vocational Education*, London: Kogan Page.

National Council for Vocational Qualifications (1993) *GNVQ Information Note*, London: NCVQ.

Smithers, A and Robinson, P (1993) *Changing Colleges – Further Education in the Market Place*, London: Council for Industry and Higher Education.

2 Preparing Submissions for Validation

Designing a successful vocational programme is a demanding task which requires the involvement of many different kinds of people who bring to the process a broad range of professional skills and knowledge. It also requires that the different participants work cooperatively as a team and not just as isolated individuals. This chapter provides practical guidance by dividing the validation process into four stages and examining some of the key competences that curriculum designers will need if they are to manage the process successfully.

An initial definition of terms may be helpful: *validation* is the process of gaining approval for a new course or programme; *re-validation* is the process of gaining approval for a replacement or modified course or programme. Both validation and re-validation involve preparing detailed documentation which is then submitted for approval to external validating bodies such as the Business and Technology Education Council (BTEC), City and Guilds or the English National Board (ENB). The processes of validation and re-validation are akin to product development and product verification in commercial organisations, in that curriculum teams are involved in the activities of designing and gaining approval for new products or courses.

Four stages in curriculum design

Preparing for validation involves four stages, which are illustrated in Figure 2.1.

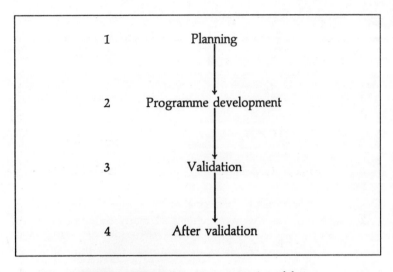

Figure 2.1 *Four stages in preparing for validation*

Stage 1: planning

It is helpful if the design team, under the direction of the programme leader, treats the submission as a project which has to be carefully managed. An investment of time in initial planning will pay enormous dividends, not least because it will create a focus for the curriculum group to come together, to start the process of team building which provides a foundation for later success. It is usually a sensible idea to work backwards from the date that the submission is due for receipt by the validation body and to identify, through an action plan, all the intervening targets that have to be met before the final deadline. It is wise to be generous with the amount allocated to the process as most teams underestimate how demanding producing a good submission can be. Figure 2.2 illustrates one approach to planning the project over a finite period of time in which the course leader and team attempt to anticipate deadlines at the start of the submission process.

Time-line		
	Task	Responsibility
Week	Example:	
1	Identifying critical deadlines – who?	
2	what? and by when?	Course team
3		
4	Select appropriate validating body for	
5	proposal	Course team
6	Send letters of notification through	
7	appropriate channels	Head of Institution
8		
9	Agree course aims and structure	Course Team
10		
11		
12	Agree document format and content	Course Team
13	Prepare first drafts	Individual
14		Colleagues
15		
16		
17		
18	Revise first drafts	Course Team
19		
20		
21	Collate first draft	Course Leader
22		
23	Print draft submission	Reprographics
24		
25	Prepare for validation meeting	Course Team
26	Internal validation meeting	Internal Panel
27		and Team
28	Amend submission	Course Leader
29		plus Team
30		
31	Submission sent off to validating body	Head of Institution
32		
33		
34	Response from validating body	Head of Institution
35		
36	Respond to conditions of approval	Course Team

Figure 2.2 *Meeting the submission deadlines*

Stage 2: programme development

During this stage, the programme team will be involved in the production of the detailed submission document. The validation requirements of the different external bodies vary but most will seek answers to the following questions:

- Why the course/programme is needed?
- What it contains; aims and objectives?
- What teaching and learning methods will be used?
- How it will be assessed and verified?
- How it will be managed?
- What quality assurance system exists?
- What human and physical resources are available?

Often the validating body will provide proformas (eg, the BTEC 'C', and 'Q' forms) for the programme team to complete. It is critical that the team carefully studies the particular guidelines for the programme and any other advice that the validating body has published. Most external bodies publish detailed guidance on such areas as assessment, APEL (Assessment of Prior Experiential Learning) policy and course implementation. The indicative list below covers the key aspects which will need to be included in a comprehensive submission.

Submission Contents

- **Factual information**
  - course/programme title and level
  - mode(s) of attendance
  - previous experience of running related courses
  - structure, including an indication of sequencing of modules and assessment.
- **Need for the programme**
  - evidence of market research
  - consultation with employers/professional bodies and evidence of their support
  - career and progression opportunities:
  - a. occupational demand for students achieving the qualification
  - b. progression to further or higher education.

- **Aims and rationale**
  - a clear set of statements which succinctly encapsulate the objectives of the course or programme.
- **Learning and assessment**
  - admission process and selection criteria including role of APEL
  - induction and student guidance
  - work experience and its relationship to the programme objectives and assessment
  - student learning experience and teaching/learning strategies
  - employer involvement in design and delivery of the programme
  - sample assignments
  - methods for monitoring students' progression through the programme
  - record of student achievement (ROA)
  - assessment strategy, methods and academic appeals procedure
  - assessment regulations, clearly specified
  - role of external verifiers/moderators and the composition of the assessment board
  - any particular provision to be made for open or distance learning.
- **Programme management and quality control**
  - clear definition of key roles, eg, programme leader, programme team, programme committee
  - composition of programme committee
  - plans for regular team meetings for planning and monitoring the programme
  - methods by which staff development needs are identified and supported
  - outline of recent staff development activities
  - description of system of quality control
  - plans for monitoring and reviewing the learning programme
  - involvement of external advisers as appropriate
  - system for referring action points to senior management
  - recent annual programme reports
  - selective commentary on external verifier/moderator reports.

- **Resources**
  Human:
  - staffing
  - CVs highlighting *relevant* recent experience and scholarly activity
  - roles of full- and part-time staff in delivering the programme
  Physical:
  - capital items
  - library and other learning resources
  - computer facilities
  - student access to resources
  - resource replacement provision.
- **Unit (or module) content**
  Common headings:
  - introduction, including rationale
  - aims
  - objectives (preferably in outcome terms)
  - content – competence, knowledge, skills, understanding, application
  - teaching and learning methods
  - assessment or performance criteria
  - resources to support learning including indicative reading list.

Student handbook
Many validation bodies will regard the student handbook as the single most important piece of evidence that the course/programme team provides to demonstrate their capacity to deliver the programme. The handbook should contain:

- welcome statement
- outline of programme structure and content
- assessment plan and assessment regulations
- procedure for academic appeals
- course/programme calendar
- course/programme team and named contacts
- book and equipment lists
- any special information relating to the course.

Stage 3: validation

There are several forms that validation can take which are a result of the differing approaches of the external validating bodies and the internal quality assurance systems that centres – schools, colleges and other training providers – operate.

Most of the national validating bodies will require the completion of detailed proformas which comprise the basis of the centre's submission. The proposal may then be validated purely on the written submission, ie, a national validation panel will meet to consider the document and reach a validation conclusion without visiting the centre. This is the approach that BTEC has historically adopted when validating BTEC First and National programmes from new and existing centres. Alternatively, the validating body may delegate the power of approval to a validation panel or group of external advisers, whose role is to visit the centre, to meet the programme team and to evaluate the suitability of the resource base for implementing the proposed programme. City and Guilds have tended to adopt the latter approach.

The validation event is often regarded by the course/ programme team with some trepidation. It represents the culmination of all the energy and work involved in developing the new curriculum and course documentation. Current thinking is to regard validation less as a form of 'examination' and more as a continuous process of curriculum development, in which the validators can enter into a constructive dialogue with the curriculum designers.

It is very rare indeed for a submission to be rejected outright by the validating body. It is much more common for the outcome to be a request for additional information or the stipulation for conditions to be met before the course/programme can commence. The following are typical outcomes:

- Approval   – no further development is needed before the course/programme commences
- Approval with   – fulfilment of recommendations is at the
  recommendations   discretion of the course/programme team, but there is usually strong

	encouragement for the centre to implement the points for action
• Approval with conditions	– fulfilment of conditions is required before the course/programme can commence and the centre is usually asked to provide additional documentation to indicate that it has met the conditions
• Non-approval	– the submission is rejected but the centre is invited to re-submit the proposal after a period of further major development.

Where centres have developed sophisticated quality assurance systems of their own, it is likely that a pre-validation event will be held before the submission document is sent to any external body. This will involve the centre setting up its own internal validation panel which will meet with the programme or course team to discuss the proposal before it progresses outside the institution. The composition of such internal validation panels will vary but it is common to include the following members:

• Chair	– normally a senior and experienced member of the centre's staff who has not been directly involved in producing the submission
• External academic	– usually from another institution which offers a similar course/programme and who has relevant subject expertise
• External employer	– often an employer with a local interest in the 'graduates' of the programme, who is therefore familiar with the employment prospects and the local market
• Internal academic	– normally from a different faculty or department, but with some experience of validation and review.

An internal validation event is a critical 'rite of passage' which allows the team members to reflect upon the proposed curriculum and demonstrates that the centre takes seriously its commitment to quality. Where schools and colleges have developed sophisticated internal systems for validation and review, it is possible that the external validating body will delegate approval and/or re-approval to the centre's own validation panel, which will then normally include a nominee or nominees of the external body. BTEC currently operates such a system of centre-based validation for particular centres and courses. This allows institutions considerable autonomy over how they validate their courses.

Stage 4: after validation

There is a tendency for course teams to regard successful validation as the culmination of the submission process. The period after successful validation is usually very hectic as the programme team re-focus their energies upon the detailed business of getting ready to teach and assess the course and to meet any conditions that the validating body has set. It is likely that the validating body will appoint an external verifier or moderator as their key contact point for programme implementation and assessment. While the verifier or moderator may have an important 'inspectorial' role in checking the assessment procedures, it is also true that the external assessor will have the brief of supporting the centre in its approach to implementing the curriculum. On NVQ and GNVQ programmes, the emphasis will be upon the structures of assessment that the centre is utilising and whether there are sufficient trained assessors and internal verifiers to operate the programme. The external verifier/moderator is thus an important source of advice to the team in the period after validation.

The competences required

It is a useful exercise for the centre's managers and the programme team to stand back from the process and to consider the competences and skills they will need to develop a successful submission. Once these have been identified clearly, they may very well form the basis of the team's initial staff development activities. Figure 2.3 demonstrates one such approach in which five areas of competence – project management, team building, meetings skills, report writing and administration – are highlighted. These are discussed in detail in the sections below.

The process	*The competences*
Planning	Project managment
Development	Team building
Validation	Meetings skills
After validation	Administration
	Report writing

Figure 2.3 *Preparing for validation. The necessary competences*

Project management

A submission is a complex product requiring careful coordination by the leader of the design team and cooperation from other participants. A project planning approach attempts to look ahead and forecast critical deadlines, key resources and likely stumbling blocks. Many commercial organisations engaged in new product development regard project management as a sophisticated process requiring well-honed skills of coordination and decision making. There is a range of techniques, such as critical path analysis, designed to facilitate successful project achievement. While it is unlikely that the curriculum design team will need such sophisticated project methods, it is none the less important for them to identify a clear action plan for the submission project which allocates responsibility for key tasks in relation to firm deadlines. Figure 2.4 illustrates one approach which can be adopted.

Action plan				
Issue needing resolution	Recommended action	By whom	By when	How

Figure 2.4 *An approach to action planning*

Team building

Virtually all the validating bodies highlight the fundamental role that the course/programme team plays in delivering a successful vocational curriculum. Most vocational courses are based upon an integrated approach which highlights central or core themes and transferable skills. Members of the course/programme team therefore need to work together very closely, particularly in such areas as the assessment of skills and the design of interdisciplinary assignments. At the curriculum planning stage, it is useful if the team can start to engage in simple team-building exercises, particularly if the centre is large and staff have many other demands upon their time. Often simple strategies such as taking members of the design team away from their normal place of work for a short period to plan their activities can bear enormous fruit. The role of the team leader as both facilitator and controller is quite critical to the success of the team as a whole. At best the submission will represent a cooperative venture in which all team members share responsibility; at worst, it will be the product of the programme leader operating in isolation from the rest of the design group.

Meetings skills

Invariably the process of curriculum planning will lead to a series of meetings between the design team members and other contributors such as representatives of employers and professional groups. Experience has demonstrated that meetings are most successful when all the participants are clear about their role and the purpose of the meeting. While this sounds patently obvious, it is striking how many meetings create frustration and fail because of an absence of such clarity. It is important therefore to consider some of the main types of meeting encountered during the submission process and their function in achieving validation. The list below offers one classification:

- Colleague
  — meetings involving people of equal status concerned with solving a shared problem, through the achievement of consensus in decision making. This type of meeting is very common during the initial stages of curriculum development when the team engages in brain-storming sessions

- Command or executive
  — highly directive, often involving a senior manager passing orders or instructions 'down the line'. Usually the person calling the meeting makes the decisions and is accountable for them. This type of meeting is rare and possibly inappropriate in submission development

- Committee
  — formal meeting with a structured agenda and minutes, often involving a range of interested groups. There will normally be a chair and secretary and rules governing procedure and behaviour. The validation event meeting, when the validators meet the course design team, usually takes this format

- Progress/review
  — report of progress made by individuals in achieving set targets, often chaired by

the team leader. Such meetings are very common in the process of curriculum development, particularly during the period immediately before validation.

In practice no single meeting will fit neatly into any one of the above categories but it is important to be aware of the range of functions that meetings serve and to make these clear to all participants. A successful submission will often represent the cumulative product of a series of different meetings.

Report writing

The written submission document is usually a fairly substantial formal report and the validating body will draw inferences about the quality of the centre and team from the quality of the documentation. It is vital therefore that attention is paid to considering the format, presentation and audience of the report. The report-writing conventions (paragraphing, presentation of data, etc.) should be agreed by all the authors who contribute to writing the document. Validating panels will have experienced the full gamut of reports, from the untidy handwritten example to the superbly edited DTP document.

Administration

Last but not least is the need for attention to administrative detail. A common fault of curriculum designers is to forget to liaise with the support staff who are likely to be involved in word-processing the document and having it printed and bound. The final document will reflect the efforts of all those involved, in whatever role, in the process.

Two examples

In practice very few centres can follow the ideal model of curriculum design described in the preceding sections. Achieving validation is merely one of many tasks facing busy institutions and it will not always be given the priority that it deserves. Individual centres will also vary greatly in the professionalism of their approach to validation. The two examples below provide cameos of centres and course teams in different institutional settings and with varying levels of experience.

Example 1

Centre 1 is an 11–18 school seeking to broaden the curriculum of its sixth form which has historically provided a diet of GCE 'A' and 'A'/S levels. The school has already had some experience of vocational programmes, through its involvement in a county CPVE (Certificate in Pre-Vocational Education) consortium made up of local schools and colleges. The governors of the school have decided to seek grant-maintained status, and the headteacher is keen to increase the staying-on rates of Year 11 pupils by offering a vocational route as an alternative or complement to 'A' level subjects.

A decision has been made to run a GNVQ Level 3 in Social Care and BTEC has been identified as the appropriate validation body. A new member of staff, Marilyn Barr, has recently been appointed to lead the new development. The school has a good reputation for providing academic courses but has had little direct experience of the quality assurance, learning or assessment approaches which underpin the vocational curriculum.

The new appointee attempts to 'get down' to the task of designing the new GNVQ programme by drawing a team of colleagues together. Problems quickly emerge, however: the 'A' level sociology and psychology teachers who form a critical part of the development team have no experience of BTEC assignment and assessment approaches. When Marilyn attempts to describe the internal and external verification procedures that underpin assessment on a vocational programme, they are quite incredulous.

The team quickly recognise that they will need a range of major staff development activities if they are to produce a coherent submission by the target date that the headteacher has set. Their time is already taken up, however, in teaching and marking and there is little space in the week for staff development.

Three months on, Marilyn has become very frustrated at the slow rate of progress. In reality she has become the major author of the document and she is becoming increasingly concerned about the capacity of the current team to deliver the GNVQ programme. Six months on and the school has decided to delay the submission for another academic year. In the meantime, resources have been prioritised for a major programme of staff development aimed at getting staff accredited as skills assessors and internal verifiers, to the Training and Development Lead Body standards (TDLB). The centre is now adopting a more focused approach to curriculum design.

Example 2

Centre 2 is a large college of further education which has had extensive experience of providing vocational courses. The college has developed an internal quality assurance system, part of which involves a system of internal validation, to approve submissions before they are sent outside the institution. There is a growing acceptance amongst teaching staff that the quality of documentation has improved as a result of this process.

The department of business studies, which already runs a number of RSA, BTEC and professional programmes, has decided to mount an NVQ Level 3 Supervisory Management programme for two local companies. Initial planning meetings have involved the company training and personnel managers who are keen on open learning study methods and validation through the National Board for Supervisory and Management Studies (NEBSM).

The programme team get to work quickly in producing their submission and rehearse their proposed responses for the internal validation panel.

At the internal validation event, however, the team, including the training managers from the local companies, are unable to answer questions from the external panel member about access to assessment, in particular how APEL will be implemented. The submission is approved subject to major development conditions which will have to be fulfilled before the document is sent to NEBSM. The team are aware that NEBSM will also send an external validator to the college, who will no doubt raise further issues.

Comment

These two examples demonstrate that designing a vocational

curriculum is a complex learning process for all involved. It is rare, and indeed perhaps undesirable, 'to get it right first time'. The demands of the external validating bodies are changing rapidly and curriculum teams need to be both well informed and extremely flexible in their approaches. The examples also show that few course teams have the luxury of standing back from the process and systematically planning their approach, as the earlier sections of this chapter have suggested. It is hoped none the less that the earlier discussion will have helped in raising awareness of some of the most common problems experienced in preparing for validation.

Summary

In this chapter an attempt has been made to describe the curriculum design process and to provide guidance to both the novice and more experienced vocational practitioner. The two examples at the end of the chapter demonstrate that there is no single right answer and that few centres, whether schools, colleges or private training providers, have a faultless process for assuring the quality of their curriculum design.

3 Designing Flexible Learning Programmes

How to design a curriculum founded upon learning programmes, rather than courses, is the most important question facing the curriculum designer in vocational education. Seeking solutions to this question raises practical questions: for example, how to deliver and assess a flexible modular curriculum. It also raises broader educational questions: for example, what is meant by the term 'flexibility' and what model of learning underpins successful practice? Given the fundamental nature of these issues, the discussion in this chapter lies at the heart of this book. An attempt will be made to first highlight the critical differences between learning programmes and courses, before considering the practical and broader issues which need to be tackled if learning programmes are to be successfully implemented.

Courses and learning programmes

The differences between the notion of a course and a learning programme have already been briefly described in Chapter 1 (see page 21). For the sake of convenience this description is reproduced below:

> The notion of a course reflects the traditional world of vocational education. A course is an integrated curriculum designed by professional educationalists, usually at a national level, by awarding or professional bodies. The course is usually delivered over a standard academic year by schools and colleges. Most

elements of the course are compulsory for students – the whole is seen as more than the sum of the parts. It is therefore unusual for the student to gain exemption from part or all of the course because of prior knowledge or experience. The pedagogical model of the curriculum is paramount, namely, that there is a recognised and authoritative body of knowledge which has to be imparted by teachers to learners in a prescribed format, in a prescribed order and over a prescribed period of time.

The notion of a learning programme challenges all these conventions. Entry and exit points for learners depend upon achievements both prior to and during the period of study. There are no in-built assumptions about the speed at which individuals can learn in order to gain credit towards a qualification. The delivery of learning programmes is not therefore constrained by the conventional academic year. Programmes are constructed using the building blocks of units or modules which represent discrete units of assessment. The whole qualification becomes the sum of the parts, in a form which is quite unlike the conventional course. In the learning programme, the cohesion and integration of knowledge and skills become a function of the learner's desire and ability to make connections between the different modules. The concept of the learning programme thus challenges the pedagogical model of the curriculum, which is based on the belief that educationalists need to design integrated courses to lead the learner progressively to an holistic perspective. In the learning programme, the student exercises choice, creates integration and negotiates learning outcomes. Learning becomes a partnership between the teacher as facilitator and the student as client.

These fundamental differences are illustrated in Figure 3.1. The preceding description and the illustration oversimplify the position; in reality, different courses vary in the degree of choice that is offered to learners. The most rigid are based upon an entirely compulsory curriculum, but the more flexible offer some choice.

Learning stage	Course	Learning programme
Before entry	The student's choice is usually between one course or another. Each course is likely to contain a pre-determined group of subjects, related to a particular occupation or profession. The student will be expected to join the course at the beginning of the academic year.	The student's choice is between different modules. These can be combined in different ways and lead to a range of qualifications in broad occupational areas. The student will be able to join the programme at a number of different points during the year.
At entry	Entry onto the course is likely to be based upon previous qualifications. The student will need guidance on the likely career implications of choosing one course rather than another. There will also be a need for subject-based induction.	Entry onto the programme will be based upon the principle of open access. The student will need extensive guidance on module choice, based upon careful diagnosis of needs and procedures for accrediting prior learning and experience. The learner will require induction into the structure of the pro-gramme and the rules governing choice of modules.
On course or on programme	The different elements of the curriculum are likely to be compulsory and delivered over a set period of time and in a set sequence. Learning styles are likely to be pedagogical. This reflects a curriculum in which there is perceived to be a body of authoritative knowledge which has to be imparted to learners by teachers in a traditional manner.	Student choice is likely to be maximised by the existence of modules, which the student can combine to achieve different qualification outcomes. Learning styles are likely to be based upon experiential models, reflecting andragogical principles in which the curriculum content is structured to reflect learner experience and some negotiation is possible.
At exit	The successful student will attain the qualification on which he or she enrolled and progress to a particular occupation or futher study.	The student will have some choice over the qualification outcome at exit. This will depend upon the module combinations successfully completed.

Figure 3.1 *The main differences between courses and learning programmes*

The reader will immediately grasp the importance of the distinction between courses and learning programmes for the development of NVQs and GNVQs. The NCVQ has firmly committed itself to developing a national framework based upon unit or modular structures, which allow the learner to accumulate and transfer credit as a result of the successful achievement of NVQ or GNVQ units. The principle on which the NVQ framework is based is that the learner should receive full recognition for prior qualifications and achievements and should not be required to repeat learning unnecessarily as a result of the restrictive regulations of particular examining bodies. Other influential bodies, such as the Further Education Unit (FEU) are also promoting credit-based learning initiatives. The curriculum design implications of credit accumulation and transfer are explored in Chapter 5.

The legacy of a course-based curriculum in vocational education is very powerful and it would be naive to imagine that the professional bodies and other interests are going to instantly embrace a flexible modular curriculum which allows students to combine elements of historically different awards. Indeed one of the interesting issues to explore further is the extent to which the NCVQ industry lead bodies (see Chapter 1, p. 17) will really permit the development of a less prescriptive curriculum.

What is flexibility?

Throughout vocational education the word 'flexibility' has crept into the jargon: flexible learning, flexible access, flexible assessment, flexible colleges and flexible management. The concept of flexibility of curriculum delivery is clearly implicit in the notion of a learning programme. Flexibility is intrinsic to the design of modular structures and flexibility is also an aspect of access, in that the student is offered many entry points to study and accreditation in the movement away from the traditional academic year. In the discussion which follows, the implications of flexibility for designing learning programmes are explored further. Three aspects of flexibility are considered: flexible organisations, flexible learning methods and flexible curriculum structures.

The flexible organisation of learning

'Flexibility of organisation' refers to the ways in which learning is managed and the manner in which resources are deployed to support learning. The successful delivery of learning programmes, as opposed to courses, requires the commitment and involvement of all staff who support learning in an institution. These include senior managers, resource unit staff, curriculum leaders, teachers and administrative staff. The concept of a learning programme directs attention to the whole of a learner's career within an institution. Thus all staff who are responsible for the way that the institution interacts with students — at entry, on programme and at exit — are responsible for the successful outcome of learning. Learning programmes have an all-pervasive impact upon the institution, in a way which is quite dissimilar from courses. The latter can often be managed perfectly effectively by individual subject-based departments.

The contrast in the institutional management structures needed for delivering learning programmes as opposed to courses, successfully, is a point that is made forcefully in the 1992 Further Education Unit (FEU) publication, *Flexible Colleges*. A course-based college is contrasted with a learner-centred college in the following way:

> A course-based college is organised around the needs of students, enrolling on courses that generally begin in September and end in the Summer term, with learning arranged in a fixed sequence, and assessment occurring at fixed points for the whole group. The learner-centred college by contrast provides an initial guidance, counselling and assessment to establish individual starting points, requirements and goals, and flexible access (ie, time, place, style/mode) to learning and assessment (FEU, 1992, p.8).

Schools and colleges committed to managing flexible learning are characterised by the following features:

- a mission and set of policies which lead to the widening of access
- the provision of resources for guidance and counselling at all the critical stages (entry, on programme and exit) of the learner's career
- enhanced market research through outreach and other activities which enable the institution to identify and respond to the needs of learners in the local community
- unit-based or modular programmes designed to accommodate the different needs of individual learners
- procedures in place for the accreditation of prior learning and experience
- resource-based open learning centres which allow the learner to learn at a pace which suits them and to develop learner independence
- information-processing systems capable of tracking individual learners as they successfully gain credit for modules completed.

These features are represented diagrammatically in Figure 3.2. Three groups of managers in the institution play a key part in developing the organisation's capacity to deliver flexible learning. These are the senior management team, the programme management team and the resource managers.

The *senior management team*, usually represented by the head and deputy heads of the school or college, will need to implement curriculum policies on student access and credit designed to support flexible learning across the whole institution. These will need to be adopted formally by the institution through the appropriate committees, such as governors and the academic board. More importantly, these policies will need to be firmly embedded in the institution's culture through appropriate staff development and dissemination practices. The policies will need to be reflected in the way in which resources are allocated to support the flexible curriculum. Most significantly, there will need to be an allocation of human and physical resources to develop comprehensive student support and guidance services and adequate resource-based learning facilities.

The team of *resource managers*, often containing the librarian,

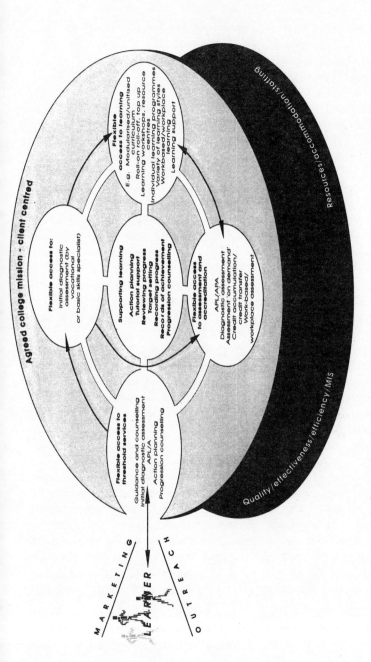

Figure 3.2 *The flexible college*

47

the computer unit manager and the senior technician, will typically develop an integrated strategy for the development of learner resources. The rapid impact of information technology has eroded traditional distinctions between printed and electronic sources of information. Many schools and colleges have already developed learning workshops, in which books and periodicals are integrated with audio-visual material and on-line computer sources. The success of such resource-based learning will depend upon how closely the resource managers work with other managers in the institution to support students on individualised learning programmes. On competence-based assignment programmes, students will work outside the classroom for much of their time and their achievements will depend upon how effectively the institution coordinates learning both inside and outside the classroom.

The *programme management team* are the group of staff most directly concerned with students. As a team, they are responsible for managing learning and assessment on the learning programme. On GNVQ and NVQ programmes, each programme team will be responsible for managing a particular occupational route consisting of a group of related vocational units. Some units, such as the core skills units, will be common to different qualifications, while others will be unique to the particular qualification. Given that the delivery style is meant to allow individual students to progress at their own pace, the need for individual student guidance and support will be critical to student success. This guidance is commonly given through tutorials linked to the student's record of achievement (ROA). Indeed the ROA plays a fundamental role on flexible learning programmes because it creates a medium through which the student can actively plan their individual learning programme in conjunction with the personal tutor. Within the team, the programme leader, commonly referred to as 'the coordinator', will play a particularly significant role. Of all the responsibilities facing the coordinator and the programme team, designing appropriate learning methods represents a most critical challenge.

Designing flexible learning methods

Perhaps the most vital principle when designing flexible learning methods is the simple recognition that no single approach will suit all learners. Learning programmes, such as NVQs and GNVQs, which are expressed in the form of behavioural outcomes, lend themselves to the use of a variety of approaches. This is because the requirement of the student is to produce evidence to satisfy the outcomes or performance criteria linked to modules. There is therefore considerable scope to use different learning and assessment tools to confirm the student's competence and a vital part of the programme team's role is to design a set of assignments which make use of the full variety of learning and assessment techniques available. Historically, one of the most fundamental characteristics of vocational courses is that the curriculum and the processes of teaching, learning and assessment have all revolved around assignments. Planning a programme of assignments which provides students with the opportunity to display their achievements against the performance criteria remains a central feature of learning on GNVQ programmes.

The benefits of a well planned assignment programme include:

- students' active involvement in the process of learning
- application of skills and knowledge to the workplace
- high levels of student motivation
- development of core skills such as numeracy, IT and communication
- development of students' capability demonstrated through such qualities as self-reliance, self-confidence and independent judgement.

As the learning programme becomes 'assignment-driven' and displays the features highlighted above, the teacher's role shifts from that of information dispenser to that of facilitator and manager of the learning and assessment process. A common misinterpretation made by staff more familiar with academic programmes, such as GCE A levels, is that vocational programmes are unstructured and unfocused because of the smaller reliance on formal teaching. The opposite is the case.

Planning a successful vocational programme requires enormous forethought and very carefully designed structures. The programme team delivering a GNVQ programme, for example, will need to have created a programme of assignments which allow the student to succeed in the following:

- the areas of knowledge which underpin the occupationally-specific units
- the personal and transferable skills embodied in the core skill units
- the additional skills and knowledge needed for success in optional units (eg, languages).

Students' achievements in each of the above will be assessed through a combination of assignments set and marked internally and external tests in some of the mandatory vocational units. (The issues relating to the assessment of vocational programmes are dealt with in Chapter 4.) Different types of assignments have been developed over many years by centres and validating bodies, to promote effective learning. The most common types of these are listed and briefly described below.

Case studies and case examples
Case studies are based upon detailed descriptions and analysis of real situations and/or incidents. As such, they are widely used on vocational programmes because they provide work-based examples which can be studied in depth by students individually or more commonly working collectively as a group. Case studies can be used to reinforce learning by applying concepts from a subject to a real example. Alternatively, they can be used to introduce a work-based problem, which is first analysed in a common sense manner. The 'common sense' evaluation can then be skilfully extended by the introduction of relevant theories and concepts from the subject discipline. A range of assignment tasks can be generated through the skilful use of case studies. Often students are allocated roles within the case study and set the task of identifying solutions to the problems faced in the real example.

Games and simulations
Simulations involve representations of reality, usually simplified

significantly to allow students to perceive the critical points. Simulations often include an element of gaming or activities involving competition or cooperation in order to achieve a set target or objective. Simulations have the enormous benefit of being manageable within the classroom or workshop. Many excellent computer-based simulations are now readily available. Simulations and games provide good opportunities for the development of interpersonal and communication skills.

Work placements and work shadowing

For full-time students on GNVQ programmes, an element of work-based assessment is normally a central feature of the programme. Colleges and schools have used a variety of methods to manage work-based learning and assessment. The work placement may be organised on one day per week or in a block during the year. The student may be based in a single department or allowed to rotate through the separate areas of the organisation. Whatever the practical arrangements, it is vital that comprehensive liaison procedures are in place between the three parties involved: the student, the employer and the tutor. In situations in which work placements are in short supply, many firms will permit other forms of work experience, of which work shadowing is one example.

Projects

Projects provide an excellent opportunity for students to develop skills in managing their own time for a major and long-term piece of work. Usually projects set on vocational courses are based upon actual work-based problems and will involve students and teaching staff making frequent visits to the organisation hosting the project. An extensive amount of information retrieval and analysis is usually also an integral feature of project work.

The above examples of assignment types are typical of the range commonly employed on vocational programmes. The role of the programme team in structuring student learning is to select an appropriate mix of assignments to allow for the development of the full range of skills and knowledge highlighted in the earlier discussion.

Flexible curriculum structures

The third aspect of designing flexible learning programmes is attention to the curriculum structure. Two features are of fundamental importance. The first is a modular curriculum which permits the accumulation of educational credit (CAT). The second is the development of a full set of institutional procedures for the accreditation of prior learning and experience (APL). These two aspects are discussed in greater detail in Chapters 5 and 6. I shall therefore confine myself in this brief section to commenting on two aspects of student learning on modular programmes – the question of integrating the content of different modules and the provision of an enhanced level of tutorial support.

Integration is commonly perceived as a key issue by programme teams. Many validating bodies such as BTEC, RSA and City and Guilds have stressed the value of a high level of integration between the different modules or components of the programme. The main reason for this emphasis is that work-based problems are seen to be intrinsically interdisciplinary in character. For example, the problems experienced by a declining business will involve an understanding of the financial, technological and human consequences of decline. A high level of integration is also seen as important in promoting student understanding. Students will see a particular subject in perspective, once they perceive the links between its subject matter and concepts derived from other disciplines. BTEC First, National and Higher National courses have developed sophisticated curriculum delivery styles for successful integration. These include the incorporation of integrated or cross-modular assignments into the assessment of the programme. Such assignments are designed to draw together the different inputs at regular intervals during the course. Designing such assignments has often proved one of the most satisfying aspects for staff working on vocational programmes.

The question of integration on learning programmes based upon separate modules, such as NVQs or GNVQs, has to be considered anew. The previous sections on flexibility have talked in terms of students negotiating their own choice of modules in a programme with many entry and exit points for learners. In other words, if the learning programme is to be truly modular, students will study at their own pace and time to achieve the learning outcomes. The programme team can no longer assume that all students on the learning programme have had the same inputs of teaching or are at the same stage of development.

On flexible learning programmes, integration becomes a function of the learner's desire and ability to make links between the subject matter of different modules. The process of integration can be facilitated by building certain design features into the learning programme. A commonly employed design strategy is to create integrated modules as compulsory elements of the curriculum, their purpose being to encourage the learner to reflect and draw together the concepts and skills learnt in the separate modules. Another possible strategy is to build in major projects as an integral feature with the explicit function of integrating the different areas of the curriculum. Qualifications accredited as NVQs or GNVQs are still based upon the student progressing within a broad occupational area. Therefore the student's learning experience will still need to be focused upon the occupation in question. Integration remains an important aim of the modular curriculum, even if it has to be achieved in different ways.

Providing students with enhanced tutorial support and guidance is also a central design issue on modular learning programmes. Students following traditional courses study as a group, usually over one or more academic years. Support and guidance are readily available from peers and from the course team who perceive the students as a regular group. Students following learning programmes are potentially more isolated. Individualised learning can imply that each student follows a unique set of modules and assignments. In practice, this degree of individuality is uncommon. Nevertheless, the concomitant of a higher degree of flexibility for the learner is the necessity for enhanced student support services.

Such student services are likely to be structured to support the student at critical points of their learning career. Usually, the stages of *induction, on programme* and *exit* are chosen by tutors as a focus for such support. Induction becomes vital for developing skills of action planning usually linked to each student's individual record of achievement (ROA). Once students grasp that success on the learning programme is dependent upon achieving the learning outcomes which form the basis of the ROA, they will recognise that effective diagnosis of strengths and weaknesses through action planning is critical.

Support for students while they are on programme will often revolve around the interim assessment stages that students experience as they progress through their individual programmes. If the learning programme is extremely flexible, students will need good basic guidance on the implications of choosing particular options. By the time students have progressed to the point of exit, further guidance will be needed for progression to higher education and different careers.

The long journey from teaching to learning

The vocational curriculum has commonly been characterised as 'student-centred'. In this final section of this chapter, I wish to briefly explore the links between flexible learning programmes and models of 'student-centredness', which are perceived to be an essential part of the successful delivery of the vocational curriculum.

Christopher Ball (1991, *Learning Pays*) makes the connection between flexibility and student-centred approaches to learning:

> What all these examples of success appear to have in common is the idea of replacing 'teacher dominated learning' with a model of flexible learning which places the needs, interests and responsibility of the student first, together with assessment which tests what can be done rather than whom is better than whom. Good education is more like health than sport.

The report, *Learning Pays*, is about the provision of lifelong learning in a society dominated by rapid economic and technological change. The stress is therefore upon styles of learning which will suit adult learners. The recognition that learning styles in post-compulsory education need to be designed for adults is critical to the successful delivery of a vocational curriculum.

Approaches to adult learning are founded upon an andrago-gical model of learning. Andragogy consists of a set of guiding principles for designing and delivering the curriculum. The most critical of these is that adult learning is self-motivated, self-directed and succeeds best when the content and style of the curriculum is related to the individual learner's work and life experience. The flexible learning methods described earlier in this chapter, such as action planning and the use of projects, reflect an andragogical approach.

As a learning theory, andragogy predates pedagogy. Pedagogy is based upon the styles of learning which are seen to be appropriate for children, namely the transmission of knowledge by adults to children through formal teacher exposition in the classroom. What are often now regarded as modern methods of teaching adults in post-compulsory education, such as case studies and simulations, have their roots in biblical and classical traditions. The learning approach used in the biblical parable is remarkably similar to that adopted in the case history. What such approaches have always recognised is that for learning to succeed the learner has to be actively involved and not merely a passive recipient of transmitted content. It is pedagogy rather than andragogy which has informed learning styles through much of the educational system. Knowles (1990) makes this point eloquently:

> Starting in the seventeenth century in Europe, schools began being organised for teaching children – primarily for preparing young boys for the priesthood.... Since the teachers in these schools had as their principal mission the indoctrination of students in the beliefs, faith and rituals of the church, they evolved a set of assumptions about learning and strategies for teaching that came to be labelled pedagogy: literally the art and science of teaching children. This model of education persisted through the ages well into the twentieth century and was the basis of our entire educational system.

Andragogical approaches have always been present in vocational education because the majority of students are adults, often studying for qualifications on a part-time basis. It is important for the curriculum designer of learning programmes to recognise the underlying model. Without this recognition, practice will be blind and ill-informed by theory. Figure 3.3 highlights the major differences between andragogy and pedagogy. The reader will recognise that features from both traditions are present in the vocational curriculum.

Pedagogy	Andragogy
Learning (teaching?) is externally directed by professional educators.	Learning is self-directed and self-rewarding.
The role of the teacher is to ensure that the teaching programme covers all elements of a set syllabus.	The role of the teacher is to act as a facilitator in enabling individuals to identify and achieve their learning aims.
Specific learning outcomes are prescribed by externally determined curricula and are related to particular career routes.	Specific learning outcomes are negotiable and often unique for each individual, the underlying goal of education being to enhance learners' capacity to continue learning.
Learning is sufficient when the goals of a prescribed curriculum are achieved.	Learning is lifelong, an intrinsic need that can never be fully satisfied.
Learning is compartmentalised into levels and subjects by external bodies. Learner choice is restricted by the compartmentalisation of knowledge.	Learning expands choice in unpredictable ways. As learners become more developed and sophisticated, they perceive new learning needs.

Figure 3.3 *Some differences between pedagogy and andragogy*

The journey from teacher-centred approaches to learner-centred approaches is a long one. There is no guarantee that learning programmes will embody the features of flexibility and andragogy discussed in this chapter. Indeed, some would argue that NCVQ has adopted a policy which is more strongly based upon pedagogy than andragogy. The well-informed curriculum designer will be aware of these issues and armed with this knowledge will design effective programmes of student learning.

Summary

The distinction between learning programmes and courses has formed the central discussion point in this chapter. An attempt has been made to unpack the concept of flexible learning and to show how flexibility is inherent in the successful delivery of learning programmes. Several examples of the design of learning programmes, including the design of NVQ and GNVQ qualifications, have been interleaved into the analysis. The implications of delivering a curriculum based upon adult learning styles have also been examined.

Further reading and references

Ball, C (1991) *Learning Pays — The role of post-compulsory education and training — Interim report*, London: Royal Society of Arts.

Business and Technology Education Council (1993) *Implementing BTEC GNVQs — A guide for centres*, London: BTEC.

City and Guilds (1993) *City and Guilds GNVQ Introductory Handbook*, London: City and Guilds.

Dewey, J (1961) *Experience and Education*, New York: Collier-Macmillan.

Further Education Unit (1992) *Flexible Colleges: Access to learning and qualifications in further education*, London: FEU.

Knowles, M (1990) *The Adult Learner - A neglected species*, 4th edn. Houston, TX: Gulf Publishing.

4 Creating the Assessment Framework

Creating a comprehensive and coherent assessment framework is one of the most daunting tasks facing the curriculum designer. Scarcely a week passes without a pronouncement about assessment from one of the National Curriculum or validating bodies. Indeed, with the introduction of standard assessment tasks (SATs) as part of the National Curriculum in the primary and secondary sectors, and the parallel development of GNVQs and NVQs for vocational courses, there has been a revolution in assessment methodologies.

In this chapter an attempt will be made to identify the critical principles which underpin good assessment practice. Practical advice will then be provided about how to develop a sound assessment strategy which incorporates clear assessment regulations and procedures for handling student appeals.

Purpose of assessment

Assessment is the process by which evidence of student achievement is obtained and evaluated. This evidence can take an infinite variety of forms, from traditional closed-book examinations to real-life projects carried out within a work setting. As far as the external validating body is concerned, the primary purpose of assessment is to enable candidates to demonstrate that they have fulfilled the objectives of the programme of study and achieved the standard for the award that they seek. From the point of view of the student and the tutor, assessment fulfils two main functions. First, it offers feedback of a *formative* kind so that the learner is better informed about his or her strengths and weaknesses and can take practical steps to improve performance. Second, it provides evidence for a grading decision which contributes to the formal assessment process. This second purpose is referred to as *summative* assessment. It is common in the early stages of vocational programmes to set a range of purely formative assignments which enable the student to gain an idea of the standard required and the expectations of the assessors. The process of summative assessment is usually encapsulated in the assessment schemes and regulations for the course or programme which provide a quasi-legalistic framework of the rules and regulations governing assessment.

What is being assessed?

The question of what it is that is being assessed is quite fundamental to the design of the overall assessment strategy of a course/programme and to the design of particular assignments or assessment tools. Most vocational courses contain a blend of three elements:

- subject-based knowledge, often described as underpinning knowledge
- skills, often referred to as core or transferable skills
- competences derived from an analysis of work-based performance.

It is the different emphasis given to these three elements by the validating body which plays the major part in determining the style of assessment that the course team adopts.

Assessment of NVQ and GNVQ programmes

The NVQ assessment model is based upon the assessment of performance in the workplace. Industry lead bodies for defined occupational areas such as management, construction and caring have established occupational standards which are derived from a functional analysis of particular job roles in an industry or sector.

These standards are broken down into units of competence which are assessed through performance criteria relating to each competence. When candidates are judged to have achieved all the elements of competence necessary for competent performance of the particular occupational role, they become eligible for the award of an NVQ. Figure 4.1 illustrates some of the key aspects of the NVQ model.

As the essence of the NVQ approach is the demonstration of observable and competent performance in the workplace, NVQ programmes have become most deeply embedded in part-time and in-company educational and training schemes such as management development or domiciliary support.

NVQ Occupational Award is broken down into
↓
NVQ Units of Competence which are broken down into
↓
NVQ Elements of Competence which are
↓
Assessed through Performance Criteria stated in outcome terms based upon
↓
Evidence which is collected to establish that the candidate displays competence in his or her occupational role
↓
This evidence may take many forms
↓

- observation of workplace activity
- observation of workplace products eg, records, reports
- testimony of others e.g. supervisors, clients
- simulations/role plays
- assessment of prior achievement
- projects
- oral questioning
- candidates' portfolios

Figure 4.1 *The NVQ competence-based assessment model*

For full-time students, the introduction of GNVQs which are more broadly based work-related qualifications, is having much greater impact. GNVQs have been developed by validating bodies to increase the participation of 16–19-year olds in full-time education, by providing a genuine alternative to traditional academic qualifications. In the assessment model of GNVQs, the emphasis is switched to units of achievement rather than units of competence and the role of knowledge in the vocational curriculum is stressed more strongly. Figure 4.2 illustrates some of these differences of emphasis.

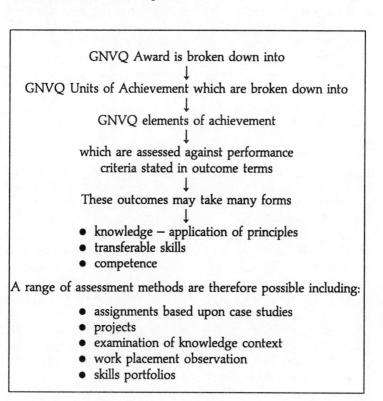

GNVQ Award is broken down into
↓
GNVQ Units of Achievement which are broken down into
↓
GNVQ elements of achievement
↓
which are assessed against performance
criteria stated in outcome terms
↓
These outcomes may take many forms
↓
- knowledge – application of principles
- transferable skills
- competence

A range of assessment methods are therefore possible including:

- assignments based upon case studies
- projects
- examination of knowledge context
- work placement observation
- skills portfolios

Figure 4.2 *The GNVQ achievement-based assessment model*

Assessment of skills

The assessment of skills – core, common or transferable – is central in most vocational programmes. Indeed, the development of skills as part of the work-related curriculum has been a feature of many initiatives such as the Technical and Vocational Educational Initiative (TVEI), Certificate in Pre-Vocational Education (CPVE), Youth Training (YT), BTEC. NVQ and GNVQ programmes also highlight the importance of skills in their approaches to assessment. Within GNVQ programmes, core skills units are now a compulsory element of the curriculum.

The classification of skills into different types varies with the validating body. Figure 4.3 illustrates the BTEC approach, which is applied to programmes at First, National and Higher levels. Other bodies, such as the National Curriculum Council (NCC), highlight some additional skills areas such as modern languages. The assessment of skills, like the assessment of competence, is usually based on explicit outcomes or a criterion-referencing approach.

The description of skills as core or transferable highlights the notion that effective skills development lies at the heart of successful achievement in all areas of the curriculum. Skills are said to be transferable because they can be applied to every aspect of work and life and they provide a foundation for developing personal effectiveness. Given their role in permeating all aspects of the vocational curriculum, the assessment of skills is invariably a course team responsibility and validating bodies will expect to find evidence that the curriculum designers have a coordinated strategy for both mapping how skills are developed across the curriculum and for recording student achievements. Most of the validating bodies provide example pro-formas (see BTEC, May 1992, for example) for maintaining a record of student achievements in different skills areas. It is also common with skills-based approaches to place a premium on the individual learner's own responsibility for keeping a log of progress and self-development. Student-centred approaches are thus common, with an emphasis upon formative rather than summative assessment.

Common Skill		Outcome
Managing and Developing Self	1:	Manage own roles and responsibilities
	2:	Manage own time in achieving objectives
	3:	Undertake personal and career development
	4:	Transfer skills gained to new and changing situations and contexts
Working with Others	5:	Treat others' values, beliefs and opinions with respect
	6:	Relate to and interact effectively with individuals and groups
	7:	Work effectively as a member of a team
Communicating	8:	Receive and respond to a variety of information
	9:	Present information in a variety of visual forms
	10:	Communicate in writing
	11:	Participate in oral and non-verbal communication
Managing Tasks and Solving Problems	12:	Use information sources
	13:	Deal with a combination of routine and non-routine tasks
	14:	Identify and solve routine and non-routine problems
Applying Numeracy	15:	Apply numerical skills and techniques
Applying Technology	16:	Use a range of technological equipment and systems
Applying Design and Creativity	17:	Apply a range of skills and techniques to develop a variety of ideas in the creation of new/modified products, services or situations
	18:	Use a range of thought processes

Figure 4.3 *The BTEC common skills outcome statement*
Source: BTEC (1992).

Underpinning knowledge and capability

For those teachers who are mainly concerned with teaching specialist subject disciplines, describing subject-based knowledge as 'underpinning' may come as something of a surprise. After all, the theories, concepts and methodologies associated with distinct specialist disciplines have historically constituted the heart of the curriculum throughout the educational system.

The idea that knowledge is underpinning is one that NCVQ have put forward because the NVQ assessment model is based upon discrete competence outcomes or measurable performance, demonstrated in a work setting. Subject-based knowledge in the NVQ paradigm clearly informs practice but is not observable in a way which can be directly measured by an assessor. There is an analogy here with crude behaviouralist models in psychology. The assessor can only make judgements based upon observed behaviour as manifested by workplace evidence. Furthermore, the domains or contexts within which this behaviour will be demonstrated are, in the NVQ model, predefined through explicit occupational standards.

A somewhat different stance is taken by the RSA Education for Capability movement (Stephenson and Weil, 1992) in which the idea of the learner's overall capability is stressed rather than particular work-based competences. Capability is viewed as an all-round human quality which involves the integration of knowledge, skills, competences and any other relevant personal attributes. The emphasis in the capability approach is on preparing learners for a changing environment by developing their independence and self-confidence. The approach to learning is therefore a holistic one: the curriculum will contain many elements – knowledge, skills and competences – but these will be integrated by every learner and by each subject discipline in a unique way which is relevant to specific learning needs. Assessment in this model will therefore reflect the unique characteristics associated with the individual's learning pro-gramme. If the learner's needs are for skills development, a portfolio approach which records the development of particular skills may be appropriate. If the individual's needs involve grasping a complex specialist discipline then more traditional academic forms of assessment may be more suitable.

The foregoing sections on competences, skills and knowledge all stress the critical importance of creating an assessment model which fits the purpose for which it has been designed. A common mistake of curriculum designers is to be unclear about the most basic question of what it is that is being assessed. If this question is not clearly considered, the assessment strategy will be fundamentally flawed.

Towards an assessment strategy

Having defined the purpose of assessment, the course team will need to consider how five key principles: accessibility, consistency, comprehensiveness, external standards and redress, can be built into a sound assessment strategy. These principles are briefly described below and then related to the practical task of creating a set of assessment regulations.

Accessibility

Perhaps the most fundamental principle of good assessment is that it should aim to be transparent. This means that the learner has right of access to all information on how he or she is to be assessed. The most common way of communicating this information to the learner is through a student handbook, which is written in user-friendly language and is made available to students before the start of the course. Chapter 2 provides details of the typical contents of a student handbook. It is worth stressing again here that such handbooks should contain details of the regulations governing assessment and student appeals.

Consistency

It should by now be self-evident that the assessment strategy and regulations need to reflect the objectives of the course or programme. It would be inconsistent, for example, for assessors to make use of a percentage-based marking system for assessing a criterion-referenced NVQ or GNVQ programme or indeed for attempting to record a student's portfolio of skills. At an early stage of course development, the programme team needs to agree a consistent approach to such issues as grading and the timing and nature of individual assessments. Most external validating bodies will provide detailed guidance on assessment and it is vitally important that the team studies this guidance carefully and agrees a common approach.

Comprehensiveness

The assessment process and regulations should endeavour to cover all eventualities. Thus the regulations should define how students will normally progress through the different stages/components of the course or programme. Procedures governing failure, referral, late submission, absence or illness should be made explicit to students. The regulations should also make clear who is responsible for different elements of assessment, when assessments are to be marked and what rights the students and assessors have.

External standards

For both the course team and the student it is important that assessment relates student achievement to the external standards required by the award. The assessment regulations should therefore encompass the requirements of the external validating body. The relationship between the assessment procedure and the external standards will normally be monitored through a process of external monitoring or verification, involving an external verifier or moderator, usually appointed by the validating body. It is important that the course team makes every effort to create clear and effective channels of communication with the moderator to ensure that the proposed assessment is compatible with the external standard.

Redress

Well-designed assessment procedures should contain precise guidance on how students can seek redress in situations where they consider there has been maladministration or injustice in the assessment process. Most of the validating bodies now require that centres clearly specify how they will handle student appeals, in a way which protects both the interests of the student and allows for neutral arbitration where conflict remains unresolved. Clearly, internal assessors will attempt to ensure that conflict is resolved long before any appeals arise by defining processes at the pre-appeal stage which avert such situations.

Drafting the assessment regulations

Ideally, the detailed regulations should reflect the five principles adumbrated above. The sub-headings below provide a checklist with hints on what and what not to include in the regulations for a typical vocational course.

1. **Achievement of the award/progression**
   - Indicate the normal rules governing how students progress from one stage of a course or programme to another and how they achieve the final award.
   - If the scheme is modular, the regulations should specify the number of modules which must be passed to achieve the award and the balance between vocational, skills and optional or additional units. If the scheme is credit-based, the regulations for achievement should be stated in credit accumulation terms.

2. **Grading of modules and assignments**
   - The grading system employed for different elements of the course should be made completely explicit. On BTEC GNVQ programmes, this will involve an overall grade for the qualification. Successful candidates will be able to achieve an overall distinction, merit or pass. On NVQ programmes, performance may be assessed on the

competent/not yet competent model and individual units will be graded separately.

3. Assessment of individual assignments and tests

- The performance criteria utilised to assess particular assignments or tests within a module or across a group of modules should be made explicit to learners. Where assessment of the qualification involves a mixture of internal and external elements, the precise balance between these modes should be made clear to students. The basis of marking, numerical or alphabetical grading, should be explained to all candidates.

4. Assessment schedule/timetable

- An assessment schedule or timetable which clearly lays out a calendar for the setting, marking and recording of assignments over the timescale of the programme should be published and included in the student handbook.
- This should include conventions for maintaining copies of assignments and deadlines for tutors to observe in returning assignments to students.
- It should also define procedures governing the late submission of course work by students.

5. Re-submission and referral

- Student rights for retrieving non-pass grades for in-course work or end tests should be clearly defined. It is common on vocational programmes to provide students with frequent access to assessment so that they can improve performance and achieve a pass grade.

6. Compensation

- If compensation is allowed within the qualification, ie, if a high level of achievement in one module can compensate for a marginal failure in another related module, this should be made clear in the regulations. It has become rare on modular credit-based programmes to allow compensation between modules because each module is regarded as a discrete unit of assessment.

7. Non-completion of assessments (in-course or examination)

- The procedures governing non-completion of in-course assessment or non-attendance at examinations should be carefully spelt out to candidates. Students' right to re-sit or re-submit assessments, with or without penalty, needs to be made absolutely clear.
- Where there are exceptional circumstances (eg, illness) the procedures governing how this is recorded need to be established.

8. Assessment board

- It is usual to establish an assessment board, at key assessment points, comprising all the internal assessors, the internal verifier and external moderator or verifier.
- The role of the assessment board is to agree student assessments for the final award and student progression from one stage of an award to another.
- The assessment board is also likely to review the success of the course through a careful analysis of the cohort data; for example, relating the number of enrolments on the programme to the number of students who achieve the final award.

9. Academic appeals

- The academic appeals procedure indicates the rights of the student to have access to an independent arbiter or set of arbiters when there is a grievance over a final assessment decision.
- Most appeals procedures will encompass a pre-appeals stage which offers the student: (i) guidance and counselling in order to avoid the formality and stress that an appeal will involve; (ii) advice on the formal process, should the student wish to pursue the appeal.
- The formal procedure will need to indicate the grounds for an appeal (for example, final grading, maladministration in the assessment process, or mitigating circumstances which were unknown to the assessors).
- The procedure will also have to identify a precise timescale and points of contact at each stage of the appeal.
- Rules governing the lodging of the appeal (normally in writing) and the maintenance of records by the parties

involved will need to be specified exactly.
- The composition of an appeals panel will need to be stipulated. This normally consists of an experienced group of colleagues who have had no contact with either the student or the assessors.
- The procedure by which appeals are heard and the sort of evidence which is admissible will need to be clarified, as will the powers of the appeals panel.
- The procedure following an appeals panel decision will also need to be defined precisely.
- The roles, if any, of external verifiers or moderators will need to be set out. It is unusual for the external verifier to be directly involved.
- The appeals procedure, or some reference to it, is normally a critical component of the student handbook.

10. Cheating and plagiarism
- The assessment regulations will need to define how the assessment board will deal with allegations or proof of cheating and plagiarism.

11. Students with disabilities
- The regulations will need to indicate what provision the centre makes for with students with disabilities so that they are not disadvantaged by the process of assessment.

12. Recognition of partial achievement
- Where it is possible to gain accreditation for elements or units of an award, common in credit-based qualifications, this should be clearly stated.

13. Role of assessors, verifier and external advisers
- The role of different parties in the assessment process needs to be defined clearly.
- For NVQ and GNVQ, the arrangements for internal and external verification of student achievement are particularly critical.

14. Accreditation of Prior Certificated Learning (APCL) or Prior Experiential Learning (APEL)
- In situations where the centre has established procedures

for accrediting prior learning, the rules governing assessment need to be carefully spelt out on such areas as the proportion of an award which can be gained through APCL or APEL.

- For NVQ and GNVQ programmes, it is essential that the centre has developed such processes of accreditation.

The foregoing section on drafting the assessment regulations shows how demanding a task this is for the programme team. It is critical, however, that the team does address this task properly, if it is to gain validation for its programme and to do justice to the needs of its students.

Levels of assessment

How to determine levels of assessment has always been one of the most problematic questions facing the curriculum designer. In this final section of the chapter, an attempt is made to discuss three perspectives on levels: the outcomes-based approach underlying NVQ and GNVQ; more traditional academic perspectives; and the capability approach, which seeks to synthesise elements of the other two.

The outcomes-based approach

The NVQ model identifies level of competence with the degree of complexity and specialisation involved in the performance of work roles. Thus an NVQ Level I will be based upon the demonstration of competence in routine and predictable work roles, while an NVQ Level IV will assume competence at a professional level involving complex technical and specialised activities.

The higher the level of the NVQ, the more it will be characterised by:

- breadth and range of competence;
- complexity and difficulty of competence;
- requirement for special skills;

- ability to undertake specialised activities;
- ability to transfer competence from one context or work environment to another;
- ability to innovate and cope with non-routine activities;
- ability to organise and plan work;
- ability to supervise others.

(NCVQ, 1989).

The ability to transfer competence from one work environment to another is particularly critical in that it closely relates to the notion of a generic ability.

NCVQ (1989) defines the first four levels in the following indicative way.

- Level 1: competence in the performance of work activities which are in the main routine and predictable or provide a broad function, primarily as a basis for progression.
- Level 2: competence in a broader and more demanding range of work activities involving greater individual responsibility and autonomy than Level I.
- Level 3: competence in skilled areas that involve performance of a broad range of work activities, including many that are complex and non-routine. In some areas, supervisory competence may be a requirement at this level.
- Level 4: competence in the performance of complex, technical, specialised and professional work activities, including those involving design, planning and problem solving, with a significant degree of personal accountability. In many areas, competence in supervision or management will be a requirement at this level.

The GNVQ approach is also based upon defining the outcomes, but these outcomes are stated in terms of the learner's achievement and preparedness for work rather than as specific occupational competences. The GNVQ levels do however mirror those of NVQs, and a similar approach to identifying level with autonomy and responsibility in a future workplace role is implicit.

Levels of knowledge and analysis

More traditional approaches to defining level in further and higher education have been based upon the analytical skills that the learner brings to bear on the subject that he or she is studying. However, academics have often been hesitant about being too prescriptive about the definition of level and have tended to sidestep the issue by relating level to the entry qualifications of students. Thus GCE A Level is defined as requiring a higher order of ability than GCSE simply because the standard entry qualifications for A level are a number of passes at GCSE; and the first year of an undergraduate degree is seen as higher than A Level because A Levels are required for entry.

Where more explicit attempts have been made to define hierarchies of academic understanding, common yardsticks, as shown in Figure 4.4, are used.

Lower

- Familiarity with subject terminology
- Evidence of relevant background reading
- Clear logical presentation
- Standard academic referencing
- Increased familiarity with technical terminology
- More detailed critical analysis and evaluation
- Synthesis of competing perspectives
- In-depth critical analysis and use of relevant research methodology
- Evidence of originality of thought

Higher

Figure 4.4 *An academic hierarchy?*

Much academic assessment on GCE A Level and degree programmes has historically been based upon a norm-referencing approach in which the standard ascribed to a candidate's performance is a function of that performance in relation to that of other comparable students. By marking a large sample of scripts, the examiner gets a feel for the standard of strong and weak candidates. In contrast, assessment on vocational programmes is more likely to be criterion-referenced, in which the standard ascribed to a candidate's performance is a function of that performance in relation to defined and pre-specified assessment criteria. The NVQ and GNVQ models are obviously strongly based upon criterion-referencing.

Capability and the capacity for independent judgement

An alternative approach which can be seen to integrate the assessment of knowledge, skills and competences is associated with the RSA Education for Capability movement (Stephenson and Weil, 1992). As outlined earlier in this chapter, capability is viewed as an all-round human quality, an integration of knowledge, skills and personal qualities used effectively and appropriately in response to varied, familiar and unfamiliar circumstances.

The capability approach is both holistic and individualistic in its assessment philosophy. It is holistic because it recognises that the learner will apply knowledge, competence and skills when tackling a specific problem. The curriculum must inevitably therefore reflect and integrate these dimensions. It is individualistic because each learner will draw upon these three areas in a way which is unique to him or her. There can therefore be no predetermined formula or prescribed range of competences for solving the complex problems that arise in a learning situation.

The key to defining level in the capability approach is the learner's capacity to take effective action in response to a context of change. The changes facing the individual may be predictable and familiar at one extreme, and unpredictable and unfamiliar at the other. In solving a given problem in a change situation, the learner will draw upon areas of knowledge, skill and competence acquired through prior experience or from structured learning programmes or courses.

Figure 4.5 illustrates two forms of capability: dependent capability in learning situations where the problem and context

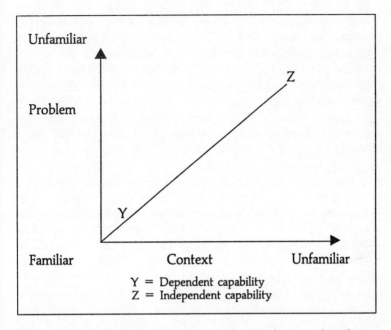

Figure 4.5 *Dependent and independent capability (Stephenson and Weil 1992)*

are well known to the learner, and independent capability in which both the problem and the environment are unfamiliar. Teachers will recognise that the simpler types of learning correspond with point Y on the graph, while more complex learning allows the achievement of point Z defined by Stephenson and Weil (1992) as independent capability, which may thus be seen as a feature of higher levels of learning.

The capability approach recognises competence as one element in learning and assessment – a necessary but not sufficient condition. Thus, to drive a car, a driver will need to demonstrate competence in the following areas, amongst others:

- insert key in ignition
- turn on engine
- place foot on clutch
- engage appropriate gear.

The achievement of a satisfactory performance in these and other competences will not of themselves allow the learner to achieve a pass in the driving test. For this to be achieved, the driver will need to apply knowledge from the Highway Code, exercise judgement in unpredictable traffic conditions and a multitude of other areas which demonstrate both capability and areas of competence. Driver capability will be increased as the individual encounters complex situations which are handled successfully.

The concept of capability is a useful approach for evaluating levels of learning and assessment. Through the concepts of dependent and independent capability, it provides a potential model for judging the level of capability the learner needs in relation to coping with change situations. The emphasis in this approach is upon the learner rather than upon an external definition of occupational standards. Level becomes a function of the sophistication of the learner, as demonstrated by his or her action and confidence in solving complex learning problems. Given the pace of economic and technological change in modern society, this approach has considerable appeal for curriculum designers as it spans the areas of skills, knowledge and competence. It also has appeal because it is inherently student-centred in its emphasis upon the all-round capability of the individual.

The fallibility of assessment

At the beginning of this chapter, assessment was described as a process by which evidence of student achievement is obtained and evaluated. Recent approaches incorporating NVQs have attempted to make the assessment of students both more trans-parent and more objective. While these are laudable aims, there may be an inherent problem in achieving both transparency and total objectivity. This is to do with the fact that the assessment process is based upon highly complex and sophisticated interactions between learners and the assessors. It is becoming increasingly evident as experience builds up with the assessment of NVQ competences that apparently unambiguous performance criteria give rise to great difficulty in the process of assessment. The example below, drawn from an NVQ Level 2 in Child Care and Education, illustrates the fallibilities to which assessment is prone.

Example

BTEC NVQ element from NVQ in Child Care and Education (Level 2)

The following example is a single element from one of the units in the above NVQ. The performance criteria are stated in the usual NVQ format for industry standards which attempt to make the criteria for assessment transparent to both the candidate and the assessor. This explicit definition of criteria is designed to make the process of assessment completely neutral and objective.

E.1.3   Maintain a reassuring environment for children

Performance Criteria

1.3.1   The warning and explanation given to children about anticipated changes to their normal environment and personnel are appropriate to their level of development and help them to cope with change.

1.3.2   Unexpected events which affect the children are clearly explained and reassurance is given appropriate to their needs.

1.3.3   Comfort objects belonging to children are readily available to them as and when requested.

1.3.4   Items for children's individual use are personalized where possible to encourage a sense of belonging.

1.3.5   The use of equipment and materials similar to those found in home situations reflects the cultural diversity of the children's backgrounds.

1.3.6   Children's particular needs/methods for helping individual children are clearly recorded and accessible to centre personnel.

RANGE   Types of environment: the physical environment; social/personal environment

Characteristics of children: those from the dominant cultural group; those from other cultural groups; those

---

> new to the setting; those whose sense of security has
> been disturbed for other reasons.
>
> Examples and definitions to clarify terms used in the range or the
> performance criteria.
>
> 1.3.1   Anticipated changes could include change of
> premises, change of staff, alterations to premises.
>
> 1.3.3   Examples of comfort objects: any toy, cloth/cover
> which a child uses as a familiar/comforting object.
>
> 1.3.4   Items could include: face-cloths, towels, potties, coat
> pegs, mugs.
>
> 1.3.5   Examples of equipment and materials: kitchen
> utensils, dressing-up clothes.

Source: NVQ Level 2 in Child Care and Education – Work in a Community Run Pre-School Group (BTEC, 1992)

Comment

In reality, assessing the candidate's competence in the above area is prone to confusion and to the subjective judgement of the assessor. For instance, it is remarkably difficult with performance criterion 1.3.1 to make judgements about the sort of explanations which will provide reassurance to young children and which will relate to their existing level of development. Experienced teachers will recognise the uniqueness of individual children and the need for subtlety and sophistication in any communication between the teacher and child. For an assessor, therefore, to arrive at a simple judgement of a student's competence against this criterion, would involve a detailed knowledge of the situation, the child, the symbolic context of any communication, etc. These latter dimensions could not be effectively encapsulated in an NVQ Level 2 competence specification. Given these factors, any assessment judgement by the assessor would need to embrace a wider situational knowledge than this performance criterion suggests and would inevitably involve elements of normative judgement.

This comment should not, however, be interpreted as a case for abandoning all attempts to specify learning outcomes which aim to make assessment transparent and fair. Well-defined outcomes are a useful aid for both the learner and the assessor. The purpose of the example is to demonstrate that there cannot be an infallible method of assessing student performance and that individual professional judgement lies at the heart of most assessment decisions.

Summary

In this chapter an attempt has been made to outline the principles underlying good assessment practice. These have then been applied to the difficult tasks of devising sound assessment strategies which incorporate regulations and procedures for dealing with academic appeals. An attempt has also been made to discuss the extremely problematic issue of how the curriculum designer can approach the definition of levels of assessment. Recent outcome-based approaches have been contrasted with more traditional forms, and the RSA capability approach has been offered as a possible way of sythesising these. Assessment has been identified as a process which relies upon sound professional practice.

Further reading and references

Barnett, R (1989) *How shall we assess them?*, London: Council for National Academic Awards' Information Services, Discussion Paper 1.

Business and Technology Education Council (1992) *Common Skills and Core Themes*, London: BTEC.

National Council for Vocational Qualifications (1989) *National Vocational Qualifications: Criteria and procedures*, London: NCVQ.

Stephenson, J and Weil, S (1992) *Quality in Learning. A capability approach in higher education*, London: Kogan Page.

Wolf, A (1993) *Assessment Issues and Problems in a Criterion-based System*, London: Further Education Unit.

5 Towards Credit-based Learning

The rapid spread of systems of credit accumulation and transfer (CAT) to post-16 education represents one of the most exciting developments in the vocational curriculum. The development of curricula expressed in a common currency of units of credit offers the opportunity of combining elements of vocational and 'academic' programmes in a manner which has historically been extremely rare. Credit offers the curriculum designer the chance to unify some of the previously insurmountable divides in the post-16 curriculum, for example between GCE A levels and NVQs. In this chapter, the critical elements of CAT are outlined and analysed in the context of the current movement towards a mass system of post-compulsory education. The implications of credit-based learning for curriculum development are then examined with numerous illustrative examples.

The building blocks of credit-based learning

In a report for the Department of Education and Science (now the Department for Education) in 1979, Peter Toyne defined credit accumulation and transfer as:

> ... essentially a process whereby qualifications, part qualifications and learning experiences are given appropriate recognition (or credit) to enable students to progress in their studies without unnecessarily having to repeat material or levels of study, to transfer from one course to another, and gain further educational experience and qualifications without undue loss of time, thereby

contributing to the maximisation of accumulated educational capital.

It is now commonly recognised that there are three critical elements or building blocks in systems of credit accumulation and transfer. The first of these is a curriculum based upon *modules*. The second is for modules to be expressed in the form of *learning outcomes* or in a language that provides the learner and the accreditation agencies with a clear statement of what the student has achieved. The third and arguably most critical element is an accepted mechanism for the student to be awarded *credit*, in recognition of the successful achievement of individual modules. In the three sections below these essential elements are discussed further.

Modules – units of learning and assessment

A module is a measurable unit of learning and assessment leading to the award of credit. A group of selected modules will normally lead to a designated qualification.

Most of the national awarding bodies break down their recognised awards into discrete parts, often referred to as elements, modules or units. BTEC divides its First, National and Higher qualifications into BTEC units or modules representing 60–80 hours of notional learning support time. A BTEC National Diploma in a particular subject area, for example Caring or Construction, is composed of a defined number of core and option modules. City and Guilds and RSA qualifications are divided into elements which can be achieved separately or accumulated into a fuller award. Qualifications accredited as NVQs or GNVQs are also broken down into mandatory optional and skills units. The existence of modular qualifications in vocational education is already widespread. The size and definitions of modules vary, however, between the different awarding bodies – a City and Guilds element does not represent the same volume of learning and assessment as a BTEC module. In other words, the modules only have a logic in terms of the broader qualifications and set of awards of which they form a part.

A critical issue when examining the nature of a particular modular curriculum is whether the modules only make sense as components of a given course or whether the modules can stand alone and be accumulated towards a range of different qualification outcomes. When the former applies, the modules are in effect being used as descriptors of separate syllabuses which only make sense as part of an holistic curriculum. This is normally defined by an awarding or accrediting body. The learner's choice is essentially still between one course of study or another and not one of accumulating chosen modules which can be employed for a range of different learning and assessment purposes. The curriculum design process is one which starts with the whole before considering the parts. This is a model which is deeply embedded in the English system of vocational quali-fications.

An alternative approach is to start from the modules and make them the critical building blocks of the curriculum; in other words, to start the process of curriculum design with the parts rather than the whole and to offer learners much greater flexibility about the qualification outcomes that different collections of modules can lead to. This is a curriculum design tradition which is common in the American system of further and higher education. It is also a process operated by a number of universities in the United Kingdom and the European Union in which students are offered a much wider choice of modules leading to degree-level qualifications. Even in such modular systems, the student's choice will be constrained by regulatory frameworks which indicate the combinations and levels of particular modules which have to be taken to achieve certain awards.

Within post-16 vocational education the scope for creating such flexible modular systems of accreditation has been severely limited by the diversity of accreditation arrangements and a history of competion between different awarding bodies. The vocational curriculum has as a consequence become a fragmented curriculum with few opportunities for students to move between the course-based qualifications offered by the major validating bodies. The development of credit-based learning is designed to overcome this fragmentation.

Learning outcomes

The expression of each module as a set of learning outcomes enables both the learner and the curriculum designer to be clear about the anticipated product of learning. Curricula expressed in the form of learning outcomes provide detailed statements of what the learner will be expected to know, understand and do upon successful completion of a module. The objectives of learning become transparent. The translation of the curriculum into outcome statements is now very common across secondary, further and higher education. The National Curriculum is stated in terms of expected pupil attainment. In a similar manner, the new intermediate and advanced GNVQs are broken down into modules expressed in terms of units of competence and associated performance criteria.

Such statements of the outcomes of learning are critical to the development of a flexible curriculum because they allow the learner much greater choice over the mode of learning and assessment. Open learning may become a possibility through the use of printed material and other media. Alternatively, the learner may decide to seek accreditation on the basis of prior learning or experience (see Chapter 6). The translation of the curriculum into modules expressed as learning outcomes creates scope for the development of more student-centred approaches.

Credit – the development of a common currency

The analogy between the concept of educational credit and a common currency is an extremely apt one. Within the economy, the currency or money fulfils the three classic functions of *a medium of exchange, a unit of account* and *a store of wealth.* The importance of a medium of exchange is that it is convertible. Money, in such forms as banknotes and cheques, allows individuals to exchange one good or service for another – for example, income earned from working into food. A generally accepted educational credit would allow learners to convert credits gained from studying modules towards different awards and qualifications.

An effective currency is highly divisible – it provides a good unit of account and an effective measure of value. Banknotes and coins, to follow this crude analogy, most obviously exhibit these features. They allow us to express the value or worth of one good in terms of another, even when the goods in question are utterly dissimilar to each other. A commonly accepted educational credit would be extremely useful because it would allow for credit to be used as a measure for quite different types of student achievement – for example, in the sciences or in the arts, in vocational or academic spheres – without the often sterile debate about whether achievement in one subject or occupational area is better or worse than another.

The analogy between money and educational credit as a store of wealth is also important. This is because it conveys the idea that learners can accumulate credit over a defined period, in the same way that money can be accumulated in a savings account. This store of educational credits can then be exchanged for a particular qualification.

The most valuable function of a currency is to create coherence and order amidst diversity. Money allows quite different producers and consumers to trade in a huge variety of goods and services. A widely accepted educational credit might create similar coherence and yet allow for the current diversity in the post-16 curriculum. This is an important theme which will be developed more fully later in this chapter.

How educational credit is defined

Educational credit is a measure of learning. All systems of credit have to tackle two fundamental aspects of measurement: how to calibrate the volume of learning that has been achieved through the successful completion of a module, and how to attribute a level to that learning. Two systems of educational credit are briefly described below: the system developed by CNAA (Council for National Academic Awards), which is in widespread use in higher education; and the system being developed for further education as a result of the FEU (Further Education Unit) project, *A Basis for Credit* (FEU, 1993).

Credit in higher education

The CNAA Credit and Accumulation Transfer (CAT) scheme was established in 1986. Although CNAA was disbanded as a result of the 1992 Further and Higher Education Act, the system of credit developed by CNAA, in partnership with a number of institutions, remains firmly in place within higher education and is being further developed by the Higher Education Quality Council.

The credit tariff outlined in Figure 5.1 is based upon using credit as a measure for years of full-time degree-level study. Each year of successfully completed study is given a rating of 120 credits. The award of credit is based upon the concept of notional learning time. In the CNAA model, it is assumed that a full-time student would spend approximately 900 hours per year on learning activities. These learning activities could include any combination of tuition, private study, workshop-based activities or other forms of learning. In this model a single unit of credit represents 7.5 hours of notional learning, calculated as follows:

1 year of full-time degree-level study = 120 credits

1 year of full-time degree-level study = 900 hours of notional learning based upon an assumed 30 hours of study over 30 weeks, ie 30 x 30 = 900

Therefore 1 credit = 900/120 or 7.5 notional hours

In practice, single credit modules are extremely unusual and most higher educational institutions have developed CAT schemes in which modules based upon 10, 15 or 20 credit modules are the most common. In situations where part-time students are studying for modules and awards, the same system of calibration is employed but the length of study for a qualification – a BA (Hons) for example – would differ. Thus a part-time student pursuing an honours degree might accumulate modules to the value of 360 credits over a period of 5 years as opposed to three years for a standard full-time degree.

Credit and Level	Award	Equivalence in full-time study
Level 1 120 credits	Certificate of Higher Education	Year 1 of full-time Bachelor's degree
Level 1 120 credits and Level 2 120 credits	Diploma of Higher Education	Year 1 and Year 2 of full-time Bachelor's degree
At least 360 credits including at least 120 at Level 3	Honours Degree	Year 1, Year 2 and Year 3 of full-time Bachelor's degree

Figure 5.1 *The CNAA credit tariff for undergraduate awards*

This system of credit-based learning has been widely adopted in higher education. It was initially most deeply embedded in former CNAA institutions such as the polytechnics, but it is now spreading more broadly across the university sector. As Figure 5.1 illustrates, an important feature of the system is the provision of staged qualifications – the certificate and diploma levels to recognise different levels of student achievement. In the CNAA system, the issue of level is dealt with pragmatically: it is a function of time and entry qualification. Level 1 is higher than GCE A level because A level is the most common entry qualification for a degree course. Level 2 is simply equated with the second year of a full-time degree. Many of the universities have established institution-wide CAT schemes which are variants of the above model.

Perhaps the most significant achievement of the CNAA system was the establishment of nationally agreed credit ratings for a range of professional and employment-related qualifications. The definition of credit equivalence in such fields as nursing and personnel has allowed adult students with work-based qualifications and experience to be awarded credit towards degree qualifications at both undergraduate and postgraduate levels. The CNAA credit system survives despite the demise of CNAA because of the flexibility it has created for both providers and learners.

A post-16 credit framework

In February 1992 the FEU published a discussion paper entitled, *A Basis for Credit* (ABC). This introduced the idea of a comprehensive post-16 framework for CAT. The proposed framework was designed to be compatible with CAT in higher education and to be sufficiently adaptable to cope with the immense diversity of vocational and academic qualifications in the post-16 sector. A number of individual colleges in the further education sector have started to use the ABC framework, but across post-16 education, CAT remains far less developed than in higher education. In the discussion below, the ABC model is described and its potential for creating a more flexible post-compulsory educational system is analysed.

A basis for credit – the proposed model
At the start of the chapter, it was suggested that all credit-based learning is based upon three elements: modules, learning outcomes and credit. These elements are all integral to the ABC framework which is based upon units of learning and assessment expressed in the form of learning outcomes; so too is the concept of notional time as a measure of credit. In the ABC system, one credit represents 30 hours of notional learning time or approximately one week of full-time study. A one-year full-time course, for example an intermediate GNVQ, would, by this measure, be calibrated as 30 credits or 900 hours of study. The ABC model is based upon similar premises to the CNAA system, with the important difference that 30 rather than 120 credits become the yardstick for a typical full-time course.

The ABC framework is ambitious because it seeks to encompass all post-16 education. It is designed to span secondary, further and higher education. The issue of defining level is crucial and on this ABC adopts a totally pragmatic approach. Seven levels, as outlined in Figure 5.2, are proposed.

	Awards	
Level	Vocational	Other
1	NVQ 1 GNVQ Foundation	National Curriculum Pre-Vocational Cert.
2	NVQ 2 GNVQ Intermediate	GCSE
3	NVQ 3 GNVQ Advanced	GCE A/AS
4	NVQ 4/5	HE Certificate
5	NVQ 4/5	HE Diploma
6	NVQ 4/5	HE Degree
7		HE Master's

Figure 5.2 *The ABC credit framework*

There are three further education levels based upon NVQ/
GNVQ Levels 1 to 3 and four levels for higher education based
upon three years of study at undergraduate level and a fourth for
postgraduate awards.

A fundamental premise upon which the ABC framework is
based is that it will only work if the key stakeholders in the
system accept it. Its future depends upon whether it is owned by
the colleges, schools and the examining and awarding bodies.
The critical issue in this acceptance is that the credit framework is
perceived as an *open system*.

ABC as an open system
The existing system of vocational qualifications is seen as a
closed system which has denied easy access and progression to
learners. It is based upon differentiation between the qualifications offered by competing examining bodies and there is little
agreement over how to define level. There are over 150
awarding bodies and over 1,700 qualifications. Each awarding
body has defined the structure and the levels of its own
qualifications. The student's choice has involved selecting a

particular qualification package, for example, GCE A levels, BTEC GNVQ or a City and Guilds Certificate. While there is considerable overlap between the content of the different awards, there has been no generally accepted way of combining elements of different awards or progressing smoothly from one qualification route to another. The learner has been denied recognised ladders and bridges between the various qualification routes. An accepted system of credit offers an interface between the different awards because it is designed to be an open system.

A Basis for Credit (FEU, 1992) defines an *open system* as a logical system which provides the means of interfacing with other systems. An open system is based upon users agreeing voluntarily to conform to the set of standards or the framework. An open system is based upon consensus and explicit support rather than upon imposition. Within industry there are numerous examples of open systems such as the QWERTY keyboard or the VHS cassette. The different firms manufacturing computers and video recorders accept the standard. An agreed credit framework based upon the ABC model could fulfil a similar function for post-compulsory education. There would be no compulsion on colleges and schools to express the different qualifications they offer in terms of credit. As more and more providers recognised the credit tariff, however, it would aquire a common currency derived from mutual interest and acceptance and it would thus facilitate flexible learning based upon credit transfer. New combinations involving modules from different qualifications such as A levels and Advanced GNVQs each attracting credit ratings, would create new opportunities for both learners and curriculum developers.

Developing a credit-based curriculum within an institution

Where CAT schemes have been adopted in higher educational institutions, the following design features have been established:

- the definition of standard-sized modules based upon a common measure of credit

- the articulation of modules in a common format based upon the use of learning outcomes
- a definition of the levels of modules and the levels of the awards available through combinations of different modules
- agreed entry, progression and exit points for students, usually based upon termly or 10-week modules, or semester or 15-week modules
- the establishment of administrative procedures and IT systems capable of keeping track of learners' progress through the system
- the development of validation, review and quality assurance procedures suitable for a modular curriculum
- the agreement of common assessment regulations governing the accumulation and transfer of credit following the successful completion of modules
- the development of institutional processes for the assessment and accreditation of prior learning (see Chapter 6)
- the embedding of suitable student guidance and support systems to allow students to progress through a flexible modular curriculum
- the establishment of local and regional credit consortia of schools, colleges and universities committed to the mutual development of credit-based learning and the progression that it offers learners (see Chapter 7).

Within further education, it is rare to find institutional CAT schemes which embody all of the above features. CAT is very much at the developmental stage. Indeed it is possible to classify institutions according to the degree to which credit-based learning has been developed employing the criteria listed above.

Embryonic CAT

Many institutions are at an early stage in the development of credit-based learning. Embryonic CAT schemes are characterised by the absence of an institutional framework exhibiting the features described above. Typically, the institution will have started to explore credit-based learning but there will be no agreed institutional policy. Flexible delivery, based upon a modular structure and multiple entry points for students, will only be available in a few subject areas or departments. Often external factors, such as the requirements of delivering NCVQ-accredited qualifications, will be the main impetus to curriculum change. The institution will not have absorbed the principles of CAT into its learning culture.

Transitional CAT

Institutions at the transitional stage of development will display some, but not all, of the features described above. There is likely to be a commitment from above – senior management – and below – course teams – eager to gain institutional support for flexible learning to facilitate curriculum development. Typically, modular credit-based curricula will have developed in a number of subjects and departments but there will be an absence of common structures at institutional level. There are likely to be disagreements between departments over such issues as module size and length. The institution will have recognised that an absence of agreed structures is constraining its further development and limiting progression for its learners.

Mature CAT

Institutions at a mature stage of development will have established all, or at least the majority, of features listed above. It is likely that the institution's academic board will have an approved credit scheme which applies to all programme areas. A credit measure such as the ABC framework will have been implemented and it is likely that the institution will be participating in a local or regional credit consortium based upon an associate or other partnership model. Most significantly, arrangements for managing the curriculum will have evolved to allow for careful tracking of students on modular programmes and guidance to them at critical transitional points. The example below illustrates these three stages of development.

Example: Catterth at the crossroads

This fictitious example is a based upon the history of CAT developments at a small tertiary college. Catterth College (1100 full-time equivalent) is situated in a small town in central England. It is the only provider of post-compulsory education in its surrounding area. There is a university – Unicat – nearby and also a local art and design college. Catterth College provides both further and adult education and has a modest GCE A level programme (312 fte) involving both 16–19 full-time students and a one-year course for adult returners. The college has five teaching departments: business studies, community education, science, catering and technology. The department of community education manages the cross-college A level programme and is also responsible for the adult and community courses which are offered in a number of adult education centres across the town. Relationships with the local university are very good and there is an established access to higher education course at the college.

Flexible and modular delivery has been a feature of the NVQ programmes in the departments of business studies and catering for the last two years. Within business studies, there is a roll-on, roll-off business administration programme based upon five-week units and enrolment throughout the college year. The modules are based upon NVQ outcome statements and students are able to gain accreditation throughout the year through a flexible assessment model. This is based upon the students completing portfolios of assessed work which is then subject to a process of internal assessment and verification. Within the catering department a similar model operates, with student assessment taking place in the college training restaurant and through local work placements.

Advanced and intermediate GNVQs have been introduced in science and business and a local project on the implementation of the GNVQ skills units has just been completed. The project director has recommended that the GNVQ skills units should be offered to all full-time students in the college on a modular basis operating throughout the year. APL is a feature of the NVQ programmes and the college has recently set up a cross-college student guidance service which has been funded by the local

Training and Enterprise Council (TEC). It is anticipated that a college-wide APL process will be in place within the year.

The vice-principal is keen on building upon the modular curriculum in the NVQ and GNVQ areas and also introducing accreditation to the students following courses at the adult education centres in the town. The college senior management team has reviewed the ABC framework and set the following 18-month targets for the phasing-in of a flexible modular curriculum, which have been supported by the academic board:

- the introduction of four GNVQ skills units as a compulsory element for all A level and equivalent full-time vocational students
- the adoption of modular GCE A level syllabuses, where possible, to facilitate linkages with elements of vocational programmes
- the development of a credit-rated FE access programme allowing students to combine vocational modules from Intermediate GNVQ programmes with GCSEs
- automatic progression rights for students on the above programme who achieve sufficient credit
- a project to investigate the feasibility of allowing students at the adult evening centres to be offered the opportunity of assessment for credit upon completion of their courses
- the achievement of a common APL process across the institution.

Eighteen months later

Despite several fierce debates at the academic board about the rigidities of a modular curriculum and the undesirability of forcing A level students to follow GNVQ skills units, the development of a credit-based curriculum has been a success at Catterth College. Full-time student feedback on the innovations has been positive and the college has received a favourable report from the Further Education Funding Council. GNVQ provision has been extended right across the full-time curriculum and the college is developing a common modular framework which will allow part-time students to study alongside full-time students on most college programmes. A learning resources centre with a wide range of open and resource-based learning packages has replaced the college library.

The senior management team is now preparing for the next phase of curriculum development which will involve adopting termly modules at NVQ Levels 1, 2 and 3 right across the college curriculum. Module descriptors based upon a common format of outcome statements have been agreed and the college calendar is being adapted to accommodate modular delivery. The college has put in place a student tracking system based upon computer records of individual student achievement expressed in credit terms.

Comment

Readers will recognise aspects of modular and credit-based development from their own institutional experience. The development of a flexible curriculum is rarely a smooth or tidy process and takes a number of years to achieve successfully. In terms of the classification of CAT development presented earlier in this chapter, Catterth College has probably only reached the transitional stage. It has introduced some modular elements into the full-time programmes but still lacks a comprehensive institutional framework.

Summary

The key factor in determining the broader development of credit-based learning in post-compulsory education is the acceptance of a national framework such as that proposed by the FEU in *A Basis for Credit*. As this chapter has indicated, CAT is well advanced in higher education because of the pioneering work of the CNAA and the widespread adoption of the CNAA model. Within the broader vocational education system, there have been many attempts to rationalise the diverse system of which the introduction of NVQs and GNVQs is the most recent. In the framework created by the 1992 Further and Higher Education Act, colleges may decide to act more innovatively and further develop access for their communities through voluntary participation in national credit-based initiatives.

Further reading and references

Further Education Unit (1992) *A Basis for Credit — Developing a post-16 credit accumulation and transfer framework*, London: FEU.

Further Education Unit (1993) *A Basis for Credit — Developing a post-16 credit accumulation and transfer framework*, London: FEU.

Further Education Unit (1993) *Discussing Credit — A collection of occasional papers relating to the FEU proposal for a post-16 credit accumulation and transfer framework*, London: FEU.

Planned Access to Learning Network (1993) 'Access to lifelong learning', papers presented at a Network Conference, Birmingham.

Nasta, T (1993) *Change through Networking in Vocational Education*, London: Kogan Page.

Toyne, P (1979) *Credit Accumulation and Transfer Systems*, London: Department of Education and Science.

6 Assessing and Accrediting Prior Learning

Designing effective procedures for assessing and accrediting prior learning (APL) is a critical part of the process of widening access to learning and assessment. For APL to be developed successfully requires action both at course level, by programme leaders concerned with giving learners credit for past learning, and at a wider institutional level, by senior managers concerned with developing more effective systems of student guidance and support. APL is an essential ingredient of the flexible curriculum and is unlikely to be successful if treated in isolation. In this chapter, detailed guidance is provided on how to develop APL policies and procedures which are related to other aspects of flexible learning and assessment.

The acronyms

Many acronyms are now in use to describe different aspects of this process; some of the most common of these are listed below:

APEL – the Assessment of Prior Experiential Learning – is the process by which appropriate experiential 'learning' is accredited. The word learning is vital here. Experience alone is not sufficient to justify a claim for accreditation. The candidate must demonstrate that learning has occurred as a result of experience gained outside the formal educational system. This experiential learning could take many forms, such as relevant work experience, instruction-based learning or training without professional certification.

APCL – the Accreditation of Prior Certificated Learning – is the process of accrediting prior certificated learning. It is closely related to the process of *exemption* because it allows the student to claim advanced standing or credit against particular components or parts of a course. The accreditation is based upon a previous qualification which the applicant claims covers similar ground to the intended course.

APLA – the Accreditation of Prior Learning and Achievement – is also commonly used as a generic term to describe the process of recognising prior competences, wherever they have been gained.

APL – the Accreditation of Prior Learning – is now most commonly used as a general term to encompass all of the above processes. It thus includes processes and policies designed for the accreditation of both experiential and certificated learning.

All the above concepts are based upon the simple idea that the formal educational process should build upon students' existing learning. The learner should not be required to repeat learning and assessment in areas in which he or she possesses existing competence. The development of APL cuts across all aspects of curriculum delivery. It is part of the admissions and induction process because prior learning will influence the point at which learners will embark upon a programme. It is part of formal assessment because learners have to demonstrate, through the collection of evidence, that they can prove their claims of prior achievement. It is also related to students' progression through formal education in that prior learning is accredited through the award of qualifications.

The context

APL has developed in the context of the movement to *access to lifelong learning*. The notion of lifelong learning is founded upon the premise that individuals learn throughout their lives, through activities at work, at home, in the community and through the formal educational system. The commitment to lifelong learning is inherent in the broader political aim of creating a *learning society* in the UK. Ball (1991) defines this mission thus:

> ... the RSA's vision ... is for a learning society in the UK. A learning society would be one in which everyone participated in education and training throughout their life. It would support them as citizens in their employment and their leisure. A learning society would also make provision to match these enhanced aspirations. The translation of national aspirations into reality cannot be achieved by government alone. It requires the co-operation, effort and enterprise of many agencies and all parts of society. (p.6).

In the same report, Ball argues that the achievement of a learning society is dependent upon educational institutions recognising where learning, and in particular adult learning, takes place. Much learning is acquired through informal networks at work and leisure. This informal learning contrasts sharply with the more structured and often teacher-centred learning offered by the formal education system. Ball states:

> ... it is a central theme ... that the best individual learning combines informal and structured experience, and is as far as possibe self-directed. Teaching is like nursing; with a little care most adults can preserve their health and continue learning on their own initiative (p.10).

The development of APL by educational providers is one way of linking structured educational experience with the prior learning gained through less formal situations. It therefore represents one way of creating access to a learning society. While APL has been developed to accredit the prior learning of adults, it is also applicable in the context of the 14–19 curriculum. There are many areas of overlap between GCSE and the emerging National Vocational Qualifications. The spread of work experience into the whole school curriculum has also led to 16-year old students developing a range of skills. It is a requirement of NVQ- and GNVQ-based qualifications that there is an effective process for accrediting both prior experiential learning and prior certificated learning.

From quite a different starting point, a wide range of industrialists and trade unions have lent their support to the National Education and Training Targets (NETTS) (see Figure 1.1, p.15). The NETTS envisage a huge expansion in the take-up of education and training opportunities during the 1990s. Public commitment to the targets has been expressed by the Confederation of British Industry, the Association of Chambers of Commerce, the Institute of Directors, the Training and Enterprise Councils (TECs) and major businesses and trade unions. APL, within this context, offers an important process for providing learners with much greater access to vocational education, because it creates a mechanism for linking learning through work with educational qualifications.

Implementation of the NETTS targets at a local level is being strongly encouraged by the TECs in England and Wales and the Local Enterprise Companies (LECs) in Scotland. The TEC-sponsored projects entitled 'Access to Assessment' are one way in which colleges, schools and other providers are being supported in developing wider opportunities for vocational education. The stress on NVQs in the NETTS targets is highly significant. The aim of the NCVQ from the outset has been to create a comprehensive system of vocational qualifications, accessible to learners throughout their lives. This commitment is encapsulated in the quote below:

> The traditional academic system is an excluding system which starts off with everybody at the age of 5 and by the age of 22 has excluded all but a very small number. The NVQ system works in the opposite way to that. It is an including system because, firstly it is a unit-based system ... secondly it is designed for lifetime learning ... there are ladders and bridges which allow people to move and to take with them the credit for what they have achieved (Hillier, Chief Executive NCVQ, 1991, p.11).

It is interesting to note that Hillier picks up the theme of lifetime learning. A commitment to developing APL is inseparable from the broader context of the commitment to opening up access to vocational education; indeed it is one of the bridges which allows people to trade in credit in the way Hillier describes. It is for this reason that APL policy cannot be successfully developed without the strategic support of senior managers in an institution. APL is but one aspect of the development of flexible learning and assessment. The discussion below picks up this theme by linking APL to Credit Accumulation and Transfer (CAT).

APL – one aspect of a flexible curriculum

The capacity of an educational provider to offer APL is dependent upon a curriculum which is modular, outcome-based and allows learners to gain credit for prior achievement. APL can thus be viewed as one aspect of the development of credit-based learning as discussed in Chapter 5. The three elements, *modules*, *credit* and *learning outcomes*, are highlighted again in the three paragraphs below.

A *module* has been described as learning in 'bite-sized chunks'. The total curriculum represented by the integrated course is broken down into discrete elements, as described in the previous chapter. It is also important to stress that a module requires assessment in 'bite-sized chunks' and assessment which can be made available to candidates, whether or not they have been through a formal learning process. This latter point is the critical one as far as the development of APL is concerned, because the essence of the APL process is accrediting learning that has occurred outside the formal educational system. It is for this reason that the TECs have recently steered funding towards 'Access to Assessment', the assumption being that institutions will be able to offer candidates assessment on a more frequent basis, normally following an APL procedure. A module therefore has come to mean an element of the vocational curriculum, expressed in terms of learning outcomes which can be assessed, with or without prior formal learning.

The concept of *credit* has been defined as follows:

> Credit is a unit of measurement. It provides a way of identifying the volume of learning outcome that has been achieved at a particular level. The credit is determined by calculating the total

amount of time (reading, open learning, experimenting, etc.) that the average notional student would require in order to achieve the stated learning outcomes (Hilton, 1993, p.46).

The availability of a credit-rated curriculum is important to APL candidates because it enables them to claim credit against elements (a GNVQ unit, for example) of particular vocational qualifications. It is more common for candidates to claim credit for one or two modules than for a whole qualification. The existence of credit means that learners should not have to waste their time by attending courses, or parts of courses, when they are already familiar with the learning outcomes.

The third and probably most critical precondition for APL is the articulation of modules in terms of *learning outcomes*. These are essential to candidates because they make the objectives of learning transparent. Historically, access to further and higher education has been denied by educationalists failing to specify clearly the objectives of courses in a language which the learner could understand. Without a syllabus expressed in outcome terms, APL is impossible to operate. Most of the validating bodies in further and higher education express their curricula in outcome terms. This is very apparent with NVQs and GNVQs in which the performance criteria are couched in terms of what the learner is expected to be able to do. Many of the newer universities have well-developed schemes for credit accumulation and transfer, and syllabuses are moving towards much more detailed statements of learning outcomes.

Qualifications which have been accredited as NVQs or GNVQs are based upon modular units expressed as collections of learning outcomes. APL procedures have to be incorporated into the delivery of these qualifications because they are founded upon the principle of access to assessment.

Implementing an institution-wide APL policy

It will be apparent that the development of APL in an institution is but one aspect of the development of a flexible curriculum. The delivery of APL can be seen as a staged process, as Figure 6.1 illustrates.

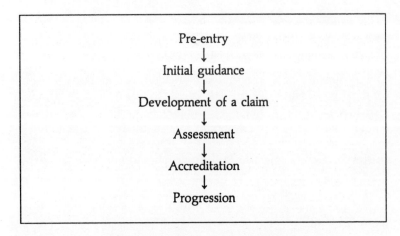

Figure 6.1 *The stages of the APL process*

Each stage is likely to involve staff at programme level, the programme leader, individual members of the course team and staff in charge of more central functions such as marketing and student services. Given the extensive level of coordination required to successfully deliver APL in different curriculum areas, it is usual to appoint a member of staff to take overall responsibility for APL across the institution, usually referred to as 'the APL coordinator'. The role of the APL coordinator is to manage the boundary between central admissions and guidance processes, and assessment and accreditation procedures, which tend to be operated at course or programme level.

Pre-entry

The pre-entry stage refers to the range of contacts between an institution and a learner that take place before the learner registers on a particular programme. It therefore includes such activities as publicity, marketing and the provision of advice about choices of course and learning methods. Given the newness of APL in many colleges and schools, developing an APL pre-entry process which successfully communicates the idea to learners is a formidable challenge.

APL was described earlier as a bridge between the learner's

prior experience and formal qualifications. For the learner, often reticent about approaching an education provider, this may be a difficult bridge to cross. Marketing, in the real sense of identifying and responding to client needs, becomes critical to successful delivery. Promoting APL to groups such as employers and adult learners is a very difficult task. The jargon associated with APL is not amenable to those most likely to benefit – adult learners. It is also unlikely that employers will immediately perceive the benefits of APL to company training programmes. Despite these problems, different providers have managed to market APL successfully.

In promotional literature it has become common to avoid the specialist jargon and to stress the benefits to learners of having their existing competence credited. Indeed 'crediting competence' is the slogan that the Management Charter Initiative (MCI), the NVQ industry lead body for management and supervisory standards, has used for promoting the idea of APL. Other authorities have used phrases such as 'adding up the past' (ENB, 1992) in the attempt to convey simply the fundamental idea.

Some providers have developed outreach centres, for example in employers' premises or adult education centres, to make APL more accessible. Clearly the creation of promotional literature is only a small first step in creating a demand for APL and the process is most likely to be successful where providers have developed effective communication channels with their local TEC and key employers. Often, significant implementation of APL occurs when there is an external demand for APL because of the requirements of the validating or professional body. This has occurred with many management programmes because of the demands of MCI. It has also occurred on many nursing courses because of the development by the English National Board of the higher award framework to recognise the continuing professional development needs of nurses and midwives.

Initial guidance

The initial guidance stage refers to the very detailed counselling and advice that institutions offer potential students who have expressed a strong interest in pursuing an APL route to assessment. Given the apparent complexity of APL, the role of professional guidance is crucial. This is typically handled by a central unit in an institution, such as student services. It is important for the institution to be absolutely clear about what purpose initial guidance serves for the learner.

The learner will normally need advice for two main reasons:

- **self-assessment** – the usual starting-point of professional guidance is to assist the learner in identifying personal strengths and weaknesses. This is commonly achieved by asking the student to complete a self-evaluation form which is designed to enable an assessment of achievements in such areas as subject knowledge, vocational competence, core/life skills and readiness for study. It is quite possible that the student will reject the APL route as a result of a detailed self-assessment process.

- **careers and educational guidance** – self-assessment is likely to be combined with a guidance interview with a professional student counsellor. The purpose of this interview is to provide objective and informed advice to enable the student to make an appropriate choice of educational programme which in turn may lead to particular career options. It is probably at this stage that APL is likely to emerge as one of the many routes to all or part of a vocational qualification.

An institutional APL policy is therefore but one aspect of a broader student guidance system. In recognition of the vital part played by good guidance, some colleges of further education have established central *access points* as a focus for APL enquiries and other requests for basic educational guidance.

At the initial guidance stage, it becomes important for staff providing the early counselling to keep in close contact with colleagues at programme level, who are likely to be involved should students decide to pursue the APL route to accreditation. Staff at programme level will be familiar with the detailed regulations and conventions regarding APL in their own occupational and subject areas. It is possible to achieve an entire qualification through APL with BTEC for example, but this may not be permitted if the qualification is validated by another body. The types of evidence that candidates will require to justify their claims for APL will also vary according to the subject or occupational area. A candidate seeking accreditation of catering competence would be likely to need different sorts of evidence to a candidate claiming skills in the accountancy area.

Development of a claim

At this stage it is assumed that, following objective and neutral advice from a student services unit, the student makes the decision to pursue an APL claim for accreditation. It is likely that students' main contacts will now be with staff at programme level with expertise in the subject or occupational area.

The candidate's success in developing an effective claim for accreditation is likely to be the outcome of three factors: first, the quality of support provided by his or her APL adviser; second, the availability of well-documented procedures for preparing the claim (an APL handbook is an invaluable aid); third, a supportive network of peers at work or in the broader community.

The *APL adviser* plays a critical role in helping candidates identify current areas of competence and in preparing and presenting evidence for assessment. It is important to be clear at the outset whether the student's claim is against prior certificated learning, prior experiential learning or a combination of the two.

As indicated earlier in the chapter, *Accreditation of Prior Certificated Learning* is concerned with giving students exemption against previous qualifications. It is important to distinguish between *general credit* and *specific credit*. General credit is that which is awarded to students for previous qualifications at the appropriate level. The previous qualification may bear no relationship at all to the future one. There is an acceptance, however, that the applicant has reached an academic level which should allow for exemption from the early stages of the qualification. Specific credit is awarded when the candidate's prior qualification is seen as being sufficiently relevant to count towards particular modules or units of the award that the candidate is seeking to gain. For example, a student intending to study for a GNVQ Level 2 qualification, with a good pass in GCSE Information Processing, might justly claim specific credit against the GNVQ core skills unit in Information Technology.

The age of the previous qualification is an important consideration in the granting of either general or specific credit. Many centres will establish regulations that specify the circumstances governing the award of credit. A common convention is to award specific credit against qualifications gained during the previous five years. The regulations governing the award of general credit tend to be more generous. There is usually a recognition that prior qualifications, at an appropriate level, are a reliable indicator of the capacity of the applicant to engage in study at a similar level.

Where the candidate wishes to pursue a claim against *prior experiential learning*, the development of appropriate evidence to support the claim is more complex. The APL adviser will normally ask the candidate to build a portfolio of evidence to present for assessment. There are two main kinds of evidence: *direct evidence* and *indirect evidence*. Direct evidence can take many forms, such as samples of work, certificates gained from a training course, and licenses. This evidence is all directly attributable to the applicant — it is a product of their own work. Indirect evidence is represented by items such as employer's letters, references, testimonials and other external comments on the candidate's achievements. The APL adviser plays the critical role of indicating to the candidate if this evidence is sufficient to justify a successful claim for accreditation.

In making this judgement the adviser will be asking the following questions:

Does the evidence match the assessment outcomes or performance criteria listed in the units of the qualification?
Is the evidence fairly comprehensive?
Are the competences and skills that the candidate has provided evidence against still current?

It is quite likely that there will be gaps in the candidate's portfolio. This will necessitate the candidate gathering further evidence through such activities as questioning colleagues at work, mini-projects to demonstrate gaps in competence and in practical subjects, and demonstrations of skills.

It is apparent from the above that the role and tasks of an APL adviser require considerable sensitivity and skill. It is for this reason that the NVQ lead body for training and development (TDLB) has specified a unit (D36) that APL advisers on certain NVQ and GNVQ qualifications are expected to gain. The business of assessment on national vocational qualifications is a complex and professional activity. Staff teaching on vocational qualifications need access to programmes of staff development which equip them effectively to discharge their new roles.

Given the detail of the evidence base needed to justify an APEL claim, a student handbook which clearly articulates the APEL process is an invaluable aid to the candidate. Typical contents of such a handbook would be:

- a simple outline of what APEL is;
- how APEL helps learners gain access to assessment and qualifications;
- an outline of the qualifications available in the institution to which APEL applies;
- the benefits and disadvantages of APEL;
- a simple explanation of the APEL procedure;
- the types of relevant evidence, with examples;
- the roles of staff in the APEL process, especially those of the assessor and the adviser;
- pen pictures of previous students who have successfully completed the APEL assessment;
- an outline of how workplace colleagues – the line manager and/or mentor – can assist with the gathering of evidence.

Any thoughts that APEL represents an easy route into vocational qualifications can be dismissed. The successful implementation of APEL requires great professionalism on the part of both student and tutor.

The third ingredient of an effective APL policy is the support of the student's workplace. In ideal circumstances the student will gain access to a mentor at work. The mentor will have a clear understanding of how vocational qualifications are assessed and will therefore be able to assist the student in identifying appropriate evidence from the organisation. He or she will also provide support and encouragement to the student, acting in the role of the critical friend. In recognition of the pivotal role played by a good mentor, many centres have developed mentor training and support networks to encourage and develop good practice. These allow supervisors and training managers from different organisations to liaise closely with staff from the centres.

Assessment

In Chapter 4, assessment was described as the process by which evidence of student achievement is obtained and evaluated. The assessment of an APL claim is a complex task because it involves looking in detail at a diverse range of direct and indirect evidence and arriving at a summative judgement about whether the candidate demonstrates sufficient achievement against the assessment criteria for accreditation to take place.

It is common practice for the assessor to be a different person from the APL adviser. This helps to ensure that the assessment is carried out objectively by a professional with no previous involvement in assisting the student to prepare the portfolio of evidence. When examining the detailed evidence, the assessor will ask the following general questions:

- **Is the evidence authentic?**
  The assessor will need to be satisfied that the blend of direct and indirect evidence provided represents a genuine record of the candidate's achievements. This can be particularly difficult to assess in situations when the sources of evidence are wide-ranging. Such evidence might include judgements made by front line assessors (a work-based supervisor, for instance), peer reports, testimonials from former employments and examples of tasks completed at work.
- **Is the evidence current?**
  In general, vocational qualifications are a demonstration of present rather than past competence. The assessor will therefore need to be satisfied that the candidate can still do what he or she claims!
- **Is the evidence sufficient?**
  The assessor's most important function is to arrive at a judgement based upon evaluating the evidence against the detailed assessment criteria for the award. The assessor will therefore consider the depth and comprehensiveness of the evidence presented.

Given the complexity of the assessment process for vocational qualifications, the TDLB has developed national standards for staff involved in the assessment of national vocational qualifications (both NVQs and GNVQs). It is a common requirement that assessors on vocational programmes should have gained TDLB unit D32 for Front Line Assessors and TDLB unit D33 for Second Line Assessors. These two units are designed to ensure that those carrying out the assessment of vocational awards have a full knowledge of the principles and the procedures of vocational assessment.

Accreditation

Accreditation is the process of providing a public record of achievement through the award of a certificate or the indication that credit is granted towards a broader qualification. Within further education, the national awarding bodies such as BTEC, RSA and City and Guilds are primarily responsible for accreditation. It is usual for the awarding bodies to appoint an external verifier to monitor the quality of the assessment procedures at a centre and to approve the issuing of certificates and diplomas which record candidates' achievements. The principle of access to assessment embodied in the APL process is now a fundamental requirement for centres wishing to offer NVQ or GNVQ qualifications. Within higher education, the universities are the main awarding bodies and where credit accumulation and transfer schemes have been fully developed, credit is usually available for APL claims.

Progression

APL is normally a means towards an end. Most commonly the student will seek to gain rapid access towards a unit or a module of a fuller qualification, rather than to complete a full qualification by APL alone. Assuming that the APL claim has been successful, the student may require further counselling about possible progression routes. As APL involves a detailed process of reflection and self-examination, it is quite possible that the student may have modified his or her original objectives.

In some cases the APL claim will not have succeeded and the candidate will require careful advice about what, if any, further evidence is needed for successful accreditation. There may be a need in some cases for some top-up learning or additional work-based experience in order to generate the additional evidence.

Implementing an APL process, involving the six stages described in the preceding paragraphs, is thus a complex and demanding process which can only succeed with cooperation from staff at both central and local levels within an institution. The illustrative example of a sixth-form college described below attempts to provide a flavour of some of the realities involved.

Example

This example is of a large sixth-form college seeking to broaden the range of its curriculum provision through the rapid introduction of intermediate and advanced vocational qualifications. The college already has a full diet of GCE A levels, GCSEs and A/S levels. It has particular strengths in the provision of science and offers the full range of physical and human sciences at GCE A level and GCSE. The college is intending to capitalise on its good reputation in science by offering BTEC Intermediate and Advanced Diplomas (GNVQ 2 and 3) in the next academic year. It believes that the style and learning methods of the GNVQs will be better suited to many of its students.

The vice-principal with responsibility for the curriculum gathers together a course design team with appropriate subject backgrounds. None of the individuals in the team has extensive experience of vocational qualifications. The main teaching and assessment expertise has been gained through a fairly traditional sixth-form curriculum. The college has, however, some experience in the provision of modular A levels and there is considerable interest in exploring modularisation further and its application in allowing students to combine elements of 'academic' and vocational programmes.

Nine months before the proposed start date for the new programmes, the course design team meet to consider the application for approval to BTEC and their immediate staff development needs. It becomes apparent that the college will need to complete BTEC 'Q' forms, for approval to run the GNVQ, and BTEC 'C' forms for approval to run NVQ- and GNVQ-based qualifications as a new BTEC centre. This documentation represents a formidable challenge as the college has not regularly been involved in the preparation of such detailed submissions.

APL only emerges as an important issue for the team through a study of the BTEC approval requirements, particularly the section on assessment in the 'C' forms. The college believes that it implements a sound access and student guidance policy. Recruitment onto the A level programmes has been based on minimum entry requirements, rather than on the stipulation of high grades or additional GCSE passes. Extensive guidance on course and career choices is also offered to all students on entry to the college. However, the notion of offering 16–19-year olds credit against previous achievements has not arisen in the past and the college does not recruit adult students.

Two members of the team are allocated the task of developing the assessment strategy for the new programme, including the APL policy. Staff development funds are made available to support their training as APL advisers and assessors over an 18-month period. These team members contact the local further education college which offers the relevant TDLB units for assessors and APL advisers. Training for these units provides the important benefit of bringing the two members of staff into contact with other training providers with experience of implementing National Vocational Qualifications. Meanwhile, other members of the team consider in detail the likely backgrounds of applicants for the new courses, in order to get an idea of the prior learning that students might claim for APL purposes. It quickly becomes apparent that many applicants could have strong grounds for accreditation of GNVQ core units on the basis of their study on previous vocational programmes at school.

Twelve months on and the college has successfully launched the new programmes. Conditional approval has been gained from BTEC and a total of 28 students are pursuing the courses. Five of these are taking part in an APL pilot at the centre to gain accreditation against the core unit in Information Processing. The external verifier has visited the centre and commented favourably on progress to date. The team is engaged in an intensive staff development programme on critical aspects of assessment such as grading on the basis of performance criteria and assessing student portfolios. Senior management at the college continue to support the initiative and there are plans to start recruiting adult students in the future.

Comment

The brief snapshot of progress at the above fictitious college is a story of considerable success. APL has only emerged as one aspect of the introduction of a vocational curriculum. Relevant training has been provided for staff and there has been support and leadership from senior management.

Vocational qualifications have only been introduced in one major area of curriculum provision. No doubt if vocational provision were to expand significantly, the centre would have to consider how it could coordinate APL across different subject areas and respond to the needs of different students, such as adult returners.

Summary

In this chapter APL has been presented as one aspect of a flexible curriculum, rather than as a policy which can be developed in isolation. APL is inextricably linked to the processes of student admissions, guidance, assessment and accreditation. It thus cuts across all the key learning processes of an institution and requires careful management if it is to be introduced successfully. Practical advice has been provided on how to implement the six stages of an institutional APL process. The development of APL has also been located in the context of the debate about expanding access to vocational education.

Further reading and references

Ball, C (1991) *Learning Pays – The role of post-compulsory education and training*, London: Royal Society of Arts.

Business and Technology Education Council (1990) *The Accreditation of Prior Learning (APL) General Guideline*, London: BTEC.

English National Board for Nursing, Midwifery and Health Visiting (1992) *Adding up the Past — APL/APEL: Guidelines for good practice*, London: ENB.

Further Education Unit (1992) *The Assessment of Prior Learning and Learner Services*, London: FEU.

Hillier, J (1991) *Vocational Qualifications for Management*, Management Charter Initiative Conference Report, London: MCI.

Hilton, A (1993) 'Credit and the Networked Learner in Higher Education' in Nasta, T, *Change through Networking in Vocational Education*, London: Kogan Page.

Management Charter Initiative (1991) *Crediting Competence — A Guide to APL for prospective licensed centres*, London: MCI.

Simosko, S (1991) *APL — A practical guide for professionals*, London: Kogan Page.

7 Partnership through Franchising

During recent years there has been a rapid growth in the franchising of vocational courses and programmes. Franchising arises when one provider, for example a college, allows another institution, such as a school or private trainer, to run a course for which it holds validation. There is a commercial aspect to franchising, in that the franchising centre normally charges a fee to the franchisee. Franchising also represents an educational partnership designed to create greater access to the vocational curriculum. Through franchising, many secondary schools are now offering vocational courses as part of sixth-form provision and many further education colleges have extended higher education provision to their local communities. In this chapter both the commercial and educational aspects of franchising are discussed and case histories are employed to illustrate some of the advantages and disadvantages of franchising.

Why franchise?

There are a number of reasons why validating bodies and different providers have become involved in the provision of courses through franchising arrangements. From the point of view of the validating body, franchising allows a relatively inexperienced provider to benefit from the expertise and guidance of a more experienced partner. The franchisee can gain from the specialisms and knowledge of the teaching and support staff of the franchising institution. It may also benefit through access to physical resources such as the library and IT facilities. Most validating bodies will expect the franchising institution to be responsible for assuring the quality of provision of the franchised course. The Business and Technology Council, for example, holds the franchiser responsible for monitoring the quality of students' learning experience in the satellite centre (BTEC, 1991). Until its demise in 1992, the Council for National Academic Awards (CNAA) also held the franchising institution responsible for maintaining the standard of the course in the institution with which it was collaborating.

From the perspective of the host institution, franchising courses to new providers creates a potentially larger market for vocational courses in its geographical area. In situations where a college enters into partnership with local schools, for instance, there is a strong likelihood that students having completed a vocational course at school will progress onto the next level of the programme at college. Where the franchise is from a college to a local company, this will provide college staff with important opportunities for updating their experience of current training practices. In situations where the host institution is a university, franchising a higher education course to a college may allow the university to extend its regional role in the area at a time when students are looking increasingly to their local college to satisfy their aspirations for HE. Franchising has resulted in much greater access to the vocational curriculum. Indeed without the spread of franchising arrangements, it is unlikely that government targets for the expansion of further and higher education could have been achieved. Somewhat ironically, networking across the secondary, further and higher educational sectors has rapidly grown just as the government has separated the funding of the three, through the creation of the Higher and Further Education Funding Councils and the varied local authority/grant maintained funding arrangements in the schools.

As far as the institution seeking to provide a course through a franchise arrangement is concerned, franchising can offer a quicker and simpler route to achieving validation than attempting an independent submission. Where the partnership operates effectively, the franchisee can build up expertise of running a vocational programme gradually and under the guidance of a more experienced centre. Tutors from the satellite institution may have access to staff development programmes at the host centre on such areas as assignment design and assessment. It is common for franchising to be perceived as a temporary arrangement – after two or three years the franchisee may feel sufficiently confident about gaining validation in its own right, having experienced the benefits of working with colleagues from the partner institution.

From the perspective of the students, franchising has led to the creation of opportunities for study in their local institution and in their local area. For adult and part-time students this extension of access has been particularly valuable. Where such students are enrolled on HE programmes in an FE college, this has eased progression onto later stages of the HE course. For full-time students in the sixth-form, the availability of franchised vocational courses has broadened the range of choices open to them and allowed for the bridging of formerly separate academic and vocational routes. It has also enabled them to benefit from contacts with the different environment of an FE college.

Types of franchise

A franchise arrangement can involve the franchising of part of a course or a complete programme. It is quite common in the early stages of a franchise partnership to allow the franchisee to run the first year of the course – the first year of a degree or BTEC GNVQ programme for example – leaving the host institution to take the students for the next stage of the course. A critical factor is the distance between the partner institutions: where they are close together, more complex patterns of cooperation – joint teaching for example – may be practical. In situations where a complete course is franchised, the franchising institution will need to be very confident that the franchisee has the necessary resources to deliver the programme.

The type of franchise will also depend upon the characteristics of the institutions in the partnership. For example, where the franchise is between a college and a school it is common for the school to be responsible for the core units in the curriculum, leaving specialist occupational units to be taught by college staff. Where the franchise involves a college and a private provider, it is likely that work-based units will be delivered by the private trainer, with the college providing students with access to the library and computing resources. When franchising partnerships develop effectively, the two institutions may choose to collaborate on more than a single programme, leading to a situation of a multiple franchise.

Franchises can also involve horizontal or vertical links. A vertical franchise is where a *superior institution* franchises a course to another provider, for example a university franchising a degree to an FE college. A horizontal franchise involves *two similar institutions*, one school franchising a course to another school, for example. It is becoming common for providers to have a range of franchise partnerships at the same time. This raises interesting questions about the capacity of the institutions to manage a complex set of different relationships.

The life cycle of a franchise

It is possible to distinguish between four stages in the life of a franchise: *negotiation, agreement, consolidation* and *termination*.

Negotiation

It is usual for the partnership to be initiated by the institution seeking to franchise a course from another provider. It is important, at this stage, that the potential franchisee has carefully thought through its strategy. The following issues should have been addressed:

- Why franchise rather than seek independent validation?
- What type of partner is most suitable (local or at some distance)?
- How will the franchised course fit within the overall portfolio of existing courses?
- Who will handle the different aspects of the franchise (fees, curriculum)?

• For how long is the franchise required?

Careful reflection upon these questions at this early stage will lead to a more professional approach to negotiation and will protect the interests of the future students.

Agreement

The formal agreement between the two institutions is usually encapsulated in a written statement or a memorandum of cooperation. This will normally include clear provisions for the following:

• how many intakes of students the franchise agreement covers
• what the responsibilities of each partner involve with respect to enrolment, registration, teaching, assessment and accreditation of students
• how the formal structures of the two institutions will interrelate with regard to appeals, course management, external verification and other aspects
• what access students and staff have to resources in both institutions, eg, library, laboratories
• what financial arrangements are applicable and when (fee per enrolment, per course, etc.)
• who is responsible for students if the partnership breaks down
• how quality of delivery will be evaluated and reported.

It is extremely likely that the franchising institution will visit the franchisee before entering into a formal agreement. Such a visit may take the form of a formal validation (see Chapter 2) with a carefully structured agenda involving meetings with senior management, the course team and an inspection of physical resources.

Consolidation

In the commercial sector, franchising normally implies that the franchisee delivers the service in almost exactly the same way as the parent institution. McDonald's sell the same beefburgers whether the franchise is in Leeds or Colchester. This is not the case with the franchising of educational courses. Each group of students and staff is unique and it is inevitable that the original course will be gradually customised and changed to suit the particular needs of the local situation. As the partnership between the two institutions matures, further development of the curriculum will be shared between the staff of the institutions. It is likely, for example, that different options will be offered to suit the needs of different employers and student groups. Different patterns of assessment may also emerge which reflect the distinct course implementation strategies of the two centres. Over time it is possible that the courses at the two centres may have grown apart to such an extent that it is time to end the partnership and seek independent validation. The ultimate test of a good franchise partnership is the ease with which it can be terminated.

Termination

As stated earlier, the memorandum of cooperation should make clear provision for the procedures which apply when the franchise agreement is ended. Where a partnership has matured in the manner described above there will often be a mutual recognition that the interests of the students and of the two institutions will be best served by separate future development. The common issue which has to be resolved is how to provide for students who have not yet completed their course. This can normally be amicably resolved through a gradual phasing out of the old programme. A much greater problem arises when there is a rift between the partners and the franchise agreement breaks down.

When franchising fails

Sadly, there are now numerous examples of the breakdown of franchise relationships. Those who stand to lose the most when the partnership falls apart are the students. The most common reasons for separation are:

● too much haste in the commencement of the franchise

- insufficient expertise at the franchising centre
- poor systems of communication
- inadequate procedures for quality control
- a lack of administrative coordination
- ill-specified financial relationships
- poor or no written agreements.

There are two common themes running through this catalogue of ills − a lack of a well-articulated strategy and deficient communication. These highlight again the critical importance of the first stage in the life cycle of a franchise − the initial negotiation. It is at this point that managers, at course and institutional level, need to invest time in building good formal and informal relationships. Franchising, like many relationships, thrives on mutual benefits − both partners need to articulate clearly what these are and how they fit into their future plans. It is also worth stressing again the importance of negotiating a tight agreement. This will prove very time-consuming but will yield enormous benefits in the long-run and particularly if the relationship deteriorates.

Franchising and other forms of association

Throughout this chapter franchising has been treated as a bilateral relationship involving one partner in allowing the other to deliver a course for which it holds validation. In fact franchising is closely related to a number of collaborative arrangements between institutions, many of which have existed for many years. These include a variety of regional consortia and associate agreements between different providers.

Historically, collaborative relationships between institutions developed in the context of local authority control of the further and secondary sectors. Thus consortia of schools and colleges operated under the umbrella of the local authority in such areas as the Training and Vocational Education Initiative (TVEI) and the Certificate in Pre-Vocational Education (CPVE). This historical pattern has now largely broken down as schools and colleges have gained increasing independence through incorporation, grant-maintained status and local management. A new pattern of voluntary cooperation between more autonomous institutions has emerged as networks of providers have created new forms of cooperation.

With the demise of CNAA, in the HE sector many universities, including the Open University, are validating degree and other courses in their regions. As a result, a number of universities have entered into associate agreements with colleges in their areas. This pattern of cooperation has coincided with an expansion of HE and the increasing tendency for students to attend their local college or university because of the financial pressures of reduced student maintenance grants. Analogous forms of association have developed between colleges and local schools in such areas as the provision of BTEC programmes. These forms of association are usually broader than franchise agreements and tend to involve far more partners and collaborative funding arrangements. The rapid spread of NVQs with the need for workplace assessment has also created networks of colleges and private trainers. The private trainers have benefited from the educational and validation expertise of the colleges, while the colleges have gained access to work placements for their students and staff.

Many of the earlier comments about the importance of clear procedures for communication apply with even greater force to such consortia. In a situation where there are many partners, the scope for misunderstandings is greater and there is a need for a commitment to a shared and well-articulated strategy by all partners, if such associations are to survive. The sub-cultures of schools, colleges and universities are significantly different and there is a need for great diplomacy and tact in the handling of the contacts between both staff and students across the participating institutions.

The commercial aspects of franchising

In no area is there greater need for clarity than in the financial relationship between the institutions. As franchising has evolved, a diversity of charging policies and procedures has emerged. It is common for the franchiser to charge the franchisee the following:

- a start-up fee for initial course development and for validation
- charge per student to cover the costs of student registration, administration and day-to-day contacts between staff at the two centres
- an amount for any specific support that the franchising centre provides, such as teaching, leading staff development sessions and attending assessment boards at the delivery centre.

The level of charging will reflect the strategy that the franchising institution is pursuing. This may involve attempting to recover all known costs and to achieve an additional return. Alternatively, the franchiser may only seek to recover the marginal costs that are incurred because it is pursuing a strategy of gaining long-term benefits from the partnership, such as increasing progression routes for learners in its area and thus eventually increasing the size of the total student enrolment. It is common for the financial charges and procedures to be summarised in a financial annexe to the memorandum of cooperation.

Two examples

In practice, franchise relationships tend to evolve in a far less systematic manner than has been described in this chapter. The two examples described below are designed to give the reader a feel for some of the realities of franchising partnerships.

Example 1

The first example involves a partnership between a school and an FE college. The secondary school is in the second term of the delivery of a BTEC First Diploma course in science through a franchise from the college. The school, an 11–18 comprehensive, is located in a relatively isolated rural area and has a small sixth form of 90 pupils. The BTEC course has been introduced to increase staying-on rates from Year 11 and to offer pupils a vocational alternative to GCE A levels. Given the poor public transport in the area, it is unusual for many 16-year olds to travel to the college, a round trip of 60 miles. Hence, the school views the introduction of vocational programmes as an important way of expanding its roll.

Initial negotiations between the school and the college in the academic year before the course commenced were handled extremely professionally. The college has gained very wide experience of working with schools through previous franchises and through participation in CPVE consortia. A joint team of staff, from the college and school, prepared the submission documentation for despatch to BTEC and there was a formal validation which involved a visit to the school from a validation panel consisting of two senior members of staff from the college and an external panel member from a school with considerable experience of running BTEC courses. This panel met the headteacher, the head of sixth, the coordinator of vocational programmes and other members of the course team. They also visited the school library and the IT resource centre. The course franchising proposal was approved, subject to an intensive staff development programme during the first year of operation of the course.

The course only recruited six students and, after a term of operation, the lecturer from the college with responsibility for liaison with the staff at the school is reporting problems in the delivery of the course. The assignments are not being assessed appropriately and the students have received little guidance on the development of common skills. Furthermore, little progress has been made in facilitating an appropriate staff development programme. These issues are raised both informally and through the course management committee which is chaired by a senior colleague from the college. Eventually there is a meeting involving the college's validation officer and the headteacher. At this meeting it is recognised that there have been teething problems with the course and the head agrees to an immediate programme of staff development in the areas of common skills and assessment.

Example 2

This example is concerned with the franchising of a management programme by a university to a group of private management consultants. The business faculty of a new university has franchised its competence-based Certificate in Management programme to a firm of private consultants which is delivering the course as part of an in-company management training scheme to first-line supervisors. All the initial arrangements for the delivery of the programme are negotiated successfully, including the financial arrangements, which are incorporated into a memorandum of cooperation.

In the early stages of the scheme, staff from the business faculty and training officers from the company are enthusiastic about the impact of the programme in raising supervisor motivation and changing the culture of the company. The participant evaluation returns also demonstrate a high level of customer and learner satisfaction.

It is at the first summative assessment point, when assessors from the company and the management consultants are challenged by the internal verifier about the sufficiency of the work-based evidence as proof of the supervisors' competence, that friction emerges. The internal verifier is the programme director at the university and she is not satisfied with the rigour and objectivity of the work-based assessment for certain candidates on the programme. Eventually the external verifier is consulted and he backs the judgement of the internal verifier.

The immediate issue is resolved, but tension has emerged in the franchise partnership. The management consultants believe that the university is imposing artificial academic standards on what they perceive to be a successful training programme. This is particularly ironic as the scheme is an NVQ competence-based programme

Comment

Both case studies illustrate some of the complexities which underlie apparently straightforward franchising relationships. Learning and assessment on vocational programmes require a high level of professional capability. Attempting to maintain high standards of quality poses the franchising institution with a range of difficult challenges. Despite these inherent problems, franchising does allow a significant extension of access to the vocational curriculum.

Summary

In this chapter the reasons for the growth in partnerships through franchising have been analysed. The different stages in the life cycle of franchise relationships have been described and practical aspects such as memoranda of cooperation and charging have been discussed. The inherent complexities of educational partnerships have been recognised in the context of the growth in access to vocational education that franchising has allowed.

Further reading and references

Business and Technology Education Council (1991) *Franchising – A guide to partnerships in programme delivery*, London: BTEC.

HMI (1991) *Higher Education in Further Education Colleges – Franchising and other forms of collaboration with polytechnics*, London: DES.

Nasta, T (1993) *Change through Networking in Vocational Education*, London: Kogan Page.

Polytechnic of North London (1992) *The Student Experience on Franchised Courses*, London: PNL.

8 Assuring the Quality of Students' Learning

Designing and implementing an effective system for assuring the quality of student learning is a complex task, which involves virtually every group: the programme team, students, administrators, senior managers, librarians, counsellors and, indeed, any other individuals who have an impact upon the learning and assessment process. Many organisations, both inside and outside education, have recently made the pursuit of quality central to their mission and to all aspects of service delivery. All the key stakeholders in vocational education, such as the NCVQ, the validating bodies (BTEC, RSA, etc.) and the Further and Higher Education Funding Councils (FEFC, HEFC) have stressed the importance of centres developing effective systems of quality control at all levels of the functioning of the institution.

In this chapter, the discussion of quality is approached at course and programme level before the broader aspects of strategic and total quality management are briefly tackled. The individual learner lies at the heart of the debate about quality and the emphasis in this discussion is on how the curriculum designer and other managers in the institution can enhance the effectiveness of individual learning, by making the pursuit of quality fundamental to the manner in which the curriculum is delivered.

Quality and the course life cycle

The notion of the course as the basic *product* of vocational education is central to most traditional systems of quality control. The concept of a *course* usually implies a curriculum that has been designed by professional educationalists, for example a course team in a school or college working within national guidelines. The course is typically delivered over a conventional academic year, is holistic in its design concept and is therefore virtually compulsory for all learners. It is implicit in the notion of a course that there is an authoritative body of knowledge which has to be imparted by teachers to learners in a certain order and over a set period of time.

The *course team* plays a central role in this model of quality control. Most of the major validating bodies such as the Business and Technology Education Council (BTEC), the English National Board (ENB) and the Institute of Personnel Management (IPM) have emphasised that it is the responsibility of the course team to design, implement and monitor the quality of the curriculum. At the course approval stage, the main focus of validation has been on the capability of the course team to deliver the proposed curriculum. The same is true of moderator and external examiner liaison, which has also focused primarily upon the relationship with the course team. This approach to the delivery of quality has fitted well with the notion that teachers and lecturers are professional groups who should have a primary concern with the effectiveness of learning and the health of the curriculum. It also reflects a sound belief that the primary responsibility for quality control should lie with the groups which are most directly involved in interacting with students.

Figure 8.1 presents the concept of the *course life cycle* – a self-perpetuating cycle of course development, validation or re-validation, approval and evaluation, leading to further development. This model reflects the discussion above – the course team designs or re-designs the vocational curriculum as an integrated whole: a carefully structured set of learning experiences for students in their care. The curriculum is presented for validation through a course submission and, following approval, is carefully monitored through student feedback and other methods. Course review and monitoring lead in turn to further curriculum development which eventually results in the need for re-validation of the programme. In the sections below, the critical

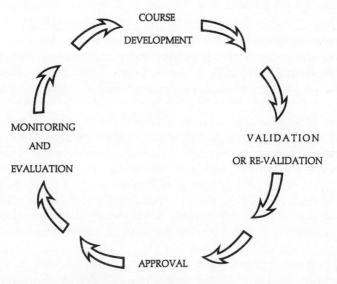

COURSE
DEVELOPMENT

VALIDATION
OR RE-VALIDATION

MONITORING
AND
EVALUATION

APPROVAL

Notes: The course team produces submission and annual review reports.
Validators interact primarily with the course team.

Figure 8.1 *Quality assurance and the course life cycle*

elements of quality assurance in this model are described fully.
Effective systems for centre-based validation and review remain
an essential part of the curriculum design process in vocational
education.

Validation and approval

The tasks related to preparing submissions for validation have
already been described in Chapter 2. The emphasis here,
therefore, is upon validation procedures as part of a centre's
process of quality control, rather than upon the role of the course
team in steering a submission to successful approval. The analogy
between product verification in a commercial setting and course
validation in an educational environment is quite a useful one.
Through a carefully structured process of course approval, the

centre is taking responsibility for the quality of the products (courses) that it is offering its clients (students). Schools, colleges and other providers are now expected to demonstrate to validating bodies (BTEC) and funding authorities (FEFC) that they have effective systems for assuring the quality of learning.

For the school or college seeking validation for a new course, part of the brief therefore is to articulate clearly how the process of course approval will operate within their institution. Systems for the internal approval of courses are deeply embedded in higher education and are becoming more common in further education. A formal procedure as illustrated in Figure 8.2 is

COURSE/PROGRAMME COMMITTEE	• annually reviews and evaluates course/programme culminating in a report and action plan • develops submission for validation, re-validation and periodic review
FACULTY/UNIT BOARDS	• receives annual course reports and critically reviews them at faculty/ unit monitoring events • reviews academic plan • approves initial course proposals • arranges validation, re-validation and periodic review events in liaison with standards committee
STANDARDS COMMITTEE	• takes an overview of review and validation across the college, advising academic board as appropriate • arranges validation, re-validation and periodic review • formulates policy in relation to quality assurance
ACADEMIC BOARD	• receives annual report from standards committee and other reports and advises as appropriate

Figure 8.2 *Quality assurance structures in a large college*

typical. This illustration shows the system of quality assurance developed in a large FE college. Each course has a course committee which includes employer and student representatives. The course committee designs and reviews the course but is itself accountable to a faculty board which overviews validation and review processes across wide subject areas such as Business or Technology. Whole institutional processes such as the validation of completely new programmes are the responsibility of a Standards Committee, which ultimately reports to the Academic Board.

The setting up of internal validation panels to approve submissions is an integral part of the above process. Such panels would normally include both internal and external members. A typical panel might comprise the following members:

- Chair — normally a senior member of management such as a head of faculty
- Two internal academic members of staff — usually from a different subject area and/or faculty
- An external academic member — usually from another institution offering a similar course/programme and with relevant subject expertise
- An external 'industrial member' — normally an employer with an interest in employing students successfully completing the course
- Committee clerk — usually a member of the registry, with experience of liaison with external bodies.

The programme for the event would be likely to involve the following meetings:

- with the *course team*, as a whole or in sub-groups, to discuss the proposed curriculum
- with *senior managers* to discuss strategic and resource issues
- with *students*, prospective, current or future, to discuss the anticipated or actual experience of the course
- with *employers* to discuss the relevance of the course content to employment needs.

The review panel would also look at the facilities such as the library, computing rooms, laboratories and workshops associated with the delivery of the course.

The following list indicates the types of questions that such panels would address to the course team:

- Are the *aims* and *objectives* of the course appropriate? Do they match the needs of the student group for whom they have been designed?
- Is there evidence of *market research*? Is it likely that students at the end of the course will have developed the necessary skills, knowledge and capabilities to cope with future employment?
- Does the *course structure* reflect the course aims? Is it well thought out and likely to provide a rich learning experience?
- What arrangements are in place for student *guidance and counselling*? What advice is provided for students at *entry*, *on programme* and *at exit*?
- What provision will be made for *tutorials*?
- How will the centre respond to the needs of students with *disabilities and/or learning difficulties*? Are such students integrated onto mainstream courses?
- What general and specialist *resources* are available to support the course? How are resources kept up to date?
- What *future developments* are envisaged for the course? Does the centre already offer courses in cognate areas?

The review panel would develop a similar agenda of questions to ask senior managers, students and employers and on the basis of this evidence would arrive at a decision on whether or not to approve the course. The range of possible validation outcomes has already been described in Chapter 2. The most common outcome is that the course is approved subject to the course team responding to certain conditions of approval.

Where centres have developed rigorous internal approval mechanisms as described above, many validating bodies are willing to delegate a substantial responsibility for validation to the centre. BTEC has developed a quality framework which grants approved centres substantial control over the validation process. Within higher education, the universities have the power of self-validation of higher national programmes. Within further education, a growing number of colleges are now operating centre-based validation, a process which allows for the validation event to take place at the college and with a panel established by the college but normally including a BTEC nominee (BTEC, 1992). With the growth of NVQ and GNVQ programmes, it is essential that the centre is able to demonstrate that it has in place institution-wide procedures of quality control. Most of the validating bodies therefore require that the centre first gains approval as an NVQ and/or GNVQ centre, before granting specific permission to offer national vocational qualifications in particular occupational areas.

The formal procedures that have been described above have developed historically, in the context of further and higher education. They therefore reflect the culture of critical peer group review and the resource base of large organisations, able to provide staff devoted exclusively to the quality assurance function. With the rapid spread of vocational programmes to secondary schools and private providers, there is a need to develop internal systems of approval which are more appropriate to both the cultures and the resources available to smaller providers.

Monitoring and evaluation

A process for the systematic monitoring and evaluation of courses is the second critical component of the model of quality assurance based upon the concept of the course life cycle. *Monitoring* involves the process of collecting quantitative and qualitative evidence about the success of the course in achieving its aims. *Evaluation* refers to the process by which the course team and others at the centre use this evidence to make judgements about the effectiveness of the course and take action to resolve problems or to further develop the curriculum. The outcome of monitoring and evaluation is usually a written report, which is normally submitted annually to an internal review group and made available to external agencies such as moderators, assessors and funding bodies. The result of regular monitoring and review is modification to the curriculum, which eventually creates a need for a full re-validation of the course. The full cycle of course development, validation, review and re-validation is illustrated in Figure 8.1

The process of course evaluation normally focuses upon three dimensions of the curriculum: quality, accessibility and validity (County of Avon, 1989). *Quality* focuses upon the internal processes of the course from the points of view of staff and students. It is concerned with such issues as the effectiveness of teaching and assessment, the adequacy of accommodation and student support.

It takes as given that the course exists and simply asks the question, how well is the course being run? The spider diagram, in Figure 8.3, illustrates the types of criteria of evaluation covered by the term 'quality'.

Accessibility focuses upon the client groups the course is serving or failing to serve. It seeks to establish how the processes of marketing and recruitment operate and whether access is denied to any particular groups in the community. The efficiency of pre-course entry guidance and counselling and the working of enrolment procedures are all aspects of access. As the spider diagram in Figure 8.4 illustrates, the central question posed is, who are we missing and why? Equal opportunities issues therefore are of prime importance.

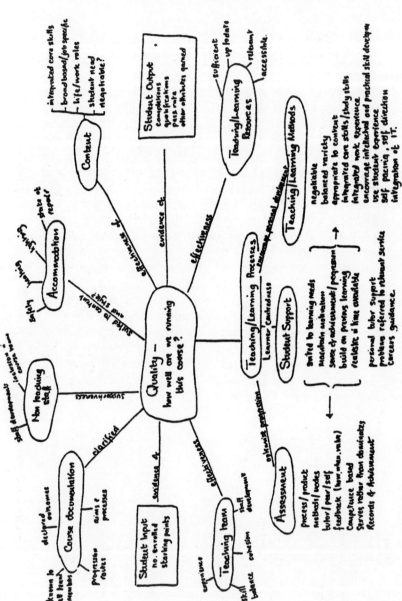

Figure 8.3 *Some aspects of quality* (County of Avon evaluation project, 1989)

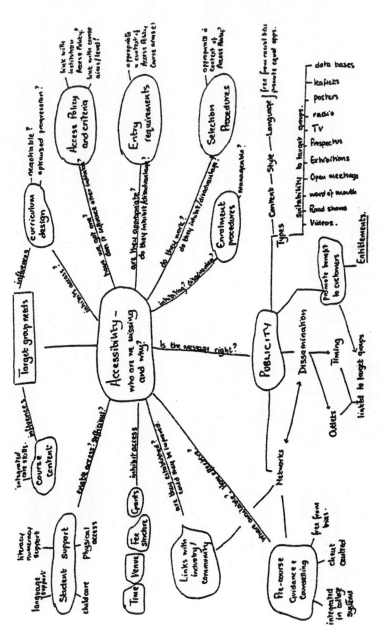

Figure 8.4 *Some aspects of accessibility* (County of Avon evaluation project, 1989)

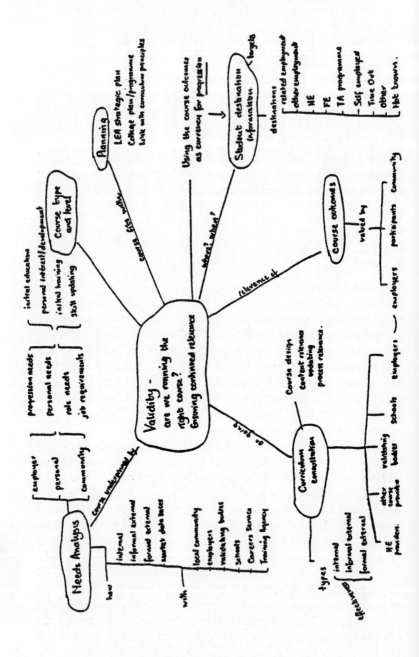

The dimension of *validity* is concerned with the occupational relevance of the course. Is it serving the needs of the industry or sector for which it has been designed? Are students developing appropriate vocational skills? Employers and professional groups play an important consultative role in answering these types of questions. The spider diagram in Figure 8.5 illustrates some of the key aspects of validity.

The Avon QAV model provides an extremely useful framework of evaluation questions. These can be applied at each stage of the life of a course:

- before entry
- at entry
- on programme
- at exit.

The course team can collect a range of quantitative and qualitative data on each of the above. Statistical records on such areas as student entry qualifications, course enquiries, completion rates and student destinations provide monitoring data, which inform evaluative judgements. Qualitative information gained through feedback from students, employers and other user groups supplements the hard data. Table 8.1 provides a few examples of these types of evidence. Readers who wish to study this area more fully are advised to refer to the further reading listed at the end of this chapter.

There is little doubt that the collection and analysis of the types of monitoring data illustrated in the table will be critical to schools and colleges wishing to attract students in the more competitive educational market emerging in the wake of the 1992 Further and Higher Education Act. Section 50 of the Act requires colleges in the further education sector, including sixth form colleges, to publish information on their students' achievements in a common format (Department for Education, 1993a). The recently published draft *Charter for Further Education* (DFE, 1993) also assumes that students and parents will have available a range of performance measures on which to base their choice of school or college. Other significant reports such as the Audit Commission/Ofsted study of full-time educational courses for 16–19 year olds, *Unfinished Business* (1993), also stress the

Table 8.1 *Examples of monitoring information related to stage of course*

Stage	Evidence	Example
1. **Before entry**	Number of applications	Centre's administrative records
	Types of applicant (age, gender, ethnicity, disability)	Application forms
	Course publicity and marketing	Course brochures, prospectus and advertising
	Pre-course guidance and counselling	Client and tutor feedback. Records of counselling sessions
2. **Entry**	Enrolment	Analysis of efficiency of enrolment procedures, waiting times, drop-in advice, etc.
	Induction	Student handbook Effectiveness of course induction arrangements
	Entry qualifications	GCSE grades, NVQ and GNVQ Records of Achievement
3. **On Programme**	Teaching and learning styles	Student and staff feedback on effectiveness of teaching and learning
	Accommodation	Quality of accommodation and room usage in relation to Department for Education norms
	Assessment	Analysis of results at assessment board and through moderator/external verifier reports

Stage	Evidence	Example
4. **Exit**	Student destinations	Analysis of student destinations, eg, full-time employment, higher education
	Qualification outcomes	Evaluation in relation to entry qualifications to measure the value added of learning
	Post-exit counselling	Post-exit interviews with samples of past students

importance of colleges and schools being able to provide systematic evidence on such areas as completion rates and the value-added element of learning, measured in terms of the additional qualifications gained through attendance and study. While these external pressures will no doubt force centres to improve their evaluation processes, the primary emphasis in this discussion has been upon the ways in which effective procedures for monitoring and review can assist centres in improving the quality of their students' learning.

From the course life cycle model to whole institutional quality frameworks

The development of effective quality systems for the approval and evaluation of courses remains an important element of centres' quality control. Recent approaches to quality assurance, however, have moved beyond the level of the course and the course team to an assessment of every aspect of the functioning of the educational organisation which has an impact upon the students learning career. The notion of the student's *learning career* is a useful one because it places an appropriate emphasis upon all the interactions that an institution has with its learners. These will commence with the first contact that the centre has with the student, for example responding to their first enquiry about the course, *before entry*. These contacts between the learner and staff will intensify *at entry*, when the student is enrolled and inducted into the course, and develop even further as the student experiences teaching, learning and assessment on his or her choosen course, at the *on programme* stage. These interactions are completed *at exit*, when the student progresses onto another course or into employment. By relating quality assurance to the notion of the learner's whole career in an institution, it becomes necessary to examine every aspect of the organisation – marketing, finance, administration and the delivery of learning – which has an impact upon the quality of the individual learning experience. This emphasis is particularly appropriate at a time when the funding bodies, the Further Education Funding Council for example, are relating the level of financial support to the capacity of colleges to retain their students to successful completion of their qualifications (FEFC, 1993).

The 'quality framework approach' is also more appropriate to a vocational curriculum founded upon credit-based modular *programmes* as opposed to courses. As the discussion in Chapter 5 indicates, individualised learning programmes are replacing courses in many subject and occupational areas. This is particularly true for colleges and schools, which have responded to the Further Education Unit's *Basis for Credit* initiative (FEU, 1993) and are well advanced in the delivery of NVQs/GNVQs. The concept of a learning programme is very different from that of a course. Flexibility of delivery is the key. In the programme, entry and exit points for learners depend upon achievement both prior to and during study. There are no in-built assumptions about the speed with which individuals can learn or about the length of time that they need to study to gain qualifications. The delivery of the programme is, therefore, not constrained by the conventional academic year. Programmes are constructed by using the building blocks of modules which are discrete units of assessment. The whole becomes the sum of the parts, and cohesion becomes a function of the learner's desire and ability to integrate the content of different modules. The concept of a programme thus implicitly challenges the role of the course team in designing an integrated and compulsory curriculum. In the programme the curriculum becomes an enabling device, which allows the learner to exercise choice and determine his or her own learning outcomes. With the development of credit-based learning, the ability of the institution to track students and guide their choice of modules becomes an important part of the process of quality control. The emphasis shifts from the single course and the course team to the totality of institutional processes: student guidance, access to assessment, the accreditation of prior learning, computer-based record systems and other procedures which facilitate effective learning.

A great deal of advice is now available to colleges, schools and other providers from the national funding, awarding and quality audit bodies about the essential elements which need to be incorporated in a total quality framework. The paragraphs below provide a resumé of some of the more recent developments.

The publication by FEFC in 1993 of *Assessing Achievement*, (FEFC, 1993a), the framework for the inspection of colleges, represents an important milestone in the debate. This approach has been viewed by many as a significant step towards a total quality management perspective for assessing the achievements of colleges. It is acknowledged in the document that quality is a dynamic concept and is related to the changing strategies of a diverse range of institutions in the new FE sector. The areas for the assessment of quality are therefore wide in scope and include the following:

- the college and its aims
- responsiveness and range of provision
- governance and management
- students' recruitment, guidance and support
- teaching and the promotion of learning
- students' achievements
- quality control
- resources.

These areas, as described comprehensively in *Assessing Achievement*, will form the basis for a four-yearly cycle of inspection visits by the FE Inspectorate. The broad emphasis in the above approach will mean that both FE and sixth form colleges will need to review carefully their strategies for improving the overall quality of their provision. There will be a need to develop quality frameworks that are much broader in scope than the traditional systems, discussed earlier, which have focused upon course approval and review.

From quite a different starting point, the validating bodies have been placing pressure on centres to provide evidence of their overall quality frameworks, particularly where the approval of NVQs/GNVQs is concerned. In 1992, BTEC introduced a system of centre approval as a prior condition for the delivery of occupationally-specific national vocational awards (BTEC, 1992). Colleges, schools and other providers now have to make an application to BTEC on 'C' forms, or centre approval forms, before being granted full approval to deliver NVQ and GNVQ awards. The 'C' forms cover the following areas:

- **Quality assurance** – including such areas as quality management with specification of roles, organisation charts and a description of monitoring procedures; internal verification arrangements and systems of communicating information to assessors and candidates.
- **Assessment** – including such areas as guidance and counselling, APL policy and procedures, records of assessment, the appeals system, and coordination of assessment sites.
- **Human resources** – including such areas as how staff training needs are identified and met and how staff development to support the assessment of NVQs is prioritised.
- **Physical resources** – including such areas as how physical resource needs are identified and met, responsibility for resource management and resource replacement.
- **Equality of opportunity** – including such areas as equal opportunities policies, their dissemination, implementation and monitoring and how access to assessment is widened for learners.

The 'C' form approach, as described here, reflects the emphasis that BTEC is placing on colleges, schools and other providers to develop whole institutional quality frameworks. For centres with well-developed internal processes, BTEC already grants a significant measure of autonomy over validation and review, as described earlier in this chapter. BTEC is thus evolving a new model for its relationship with centres which acknowledges that many have effective internal mechanisms for quality control and therefore are quite capable of making their own arrangements to assure the quality of their provision.

Many providers have already responded to the developments described above by establishing institutional-wide procedures to improve the quality of their students' learning experience. The North West Quality Network, a group of colleges in the North-West region, has worked collaboratively on a project and developed a quality framework which attempts to tackle issues of institutional quality control. The framework is designed to be sufficiently flexible, coherent and comprehensive to meet the needs of different educational providers. The project report defines explicitly the desirable characteristics of a high quality provider so that institutions employing the framework can use it as the basis for self-evaluation. The characteristics of a quality college are defined in four sections:

- People – students
- People – staff
- Resources
- Policy and management.

Each of these four areas contains a series of detailed quality statements and performance criteria which can be applied during the process of self-evaluation. This approach is illustrated in the extract shown in Figure 8.6. The process of self-critical evaluation is important and useful, particularly at a time when the major funding bodies are encouraging a process of self-assessment.

A few colleges and several private training providers have adapted industrial models of quality control such as British Standard BS5750 and Investors in People. BS5750 (and ISO 9002, its international equivalent) is based upon standards designed for manufacturing firms. These are intended to ensure that organisations have a set of comprehensive and explicit procedures for assuring the quality of service delivery for clients. To gain the standard, organisations have to undergo a process of rigorous inspection by the British Standards Institute. A checklist approach is adopted to assess the effectiveness of organisational procedures for handling such functions as

QUALITY STATEMENT	QUALITY CRITERIA	EVIDENCE	GRADE	ACTION
A1) Pre-Enrolment Information There is clear, accurate and comprehensive information about learning and assessment programmes.	a) There is a written admissions policy recognised by all staff. b) There is access to initial diagnostic assessment. c) There is written current information on all college programmes and facilities. d) All information demonstrates a clear commitment to Equal Opportunities. e) There is more detailed and accurate information on programmes to include: entry requirements, content and style, assessment, career prospects, progression opportunities and additional costs to students. f) There is clear and accurate information on Assessment/ Accreditation of Prior Learning/ Achievement (APL/A) on offer. g) There is periodic review and modification of all pre-enrolment information. h) Users are satisfied with pre-enrolment service. (A minimal level of 70%. Over 90% will be considered exemplary practice).			
A2) Admissions The admission system is responsive and efficient.	a) There is a defined timescale for responding to enquiries and applications. b) There are defined written criteria for fair selection which are consistent with the college's equal opportunities policy. c) The interview procedures are consistent with the college's equal opportunities policy. d) The admissions system is monitored and reviewed.			

Figure 8.6 A quality framework ('Section A: People – students')

purchasing, testing product quality and client response. Some colleges have successfully translated the BS5750 principles, which are couched in commercial terms, into the language of vocational education in order to evaluate the whole or particular sub-sets of the institution such as the college company.

A rather different external kitemark, Investors in People is strongly encouraged by the Training and Enterprise Councils. Investors in People is a national initiative, sponsored by the Department of Employment, aimed at improving the competitiveness of British industry by enhancing the skills of the workforce. It is predicated on the belief that the capability of staff represents the most vital resource of any organisation. This is particularly true of educational organisations which, despite the introduction of teaching technology, are still labour-intensive The standard has been incorporated into the National Education and Training Targets which aim for 50 per cent of medium to large organisations being Investors in People by 1996.

The standard comprises four key principles, as illustrated in Figure 8.7. To achieve Investor in People status, organisations have to go through a four-stage process of diagnosis, action planning, implementation and assessment. The process is designed to enable managers in the institution to evaluate the effectiveness of the communication and staff development policies, through a self-critical and structured review. When the organisation feels sufficiently confident about these processes, it invites external evaluators, appointed by the local Training and Enterprise Council, to assess the quality of the human resource management in the organisation. If the external assessment is positive, the institution gains the IIP award.

Summary

This chapter has provided a brief survey of this complex and changing area. It has evaluated quality control processes at the course and programme level before examining the development of wider institutional frameworks. Wherever possible, practical applications of quality control have been analysed. There is

An Investor in People makes a public commitment from the top to develop all employees to achieve its business objectives

i   Every employer should have a written but flexible plan which sets out business goals and targets, considers how employees will contribute to achieving the plan and specifies how development needs in particular will be assessed and met.

ii Management should develop and communicate to all employees a vision of where the organisation is going and the contribution employees will make to its success, involving employee representatives as appropriate.

An Investor in People regularly reviews the training and development needs of all employees

i   The resources for training and developing employees should be clearly identified in the business plan.

ii Managers should be responsible for regularly agreeing training and development needs with each employee in the context of business objectives, setting targets and standards linked, where appropriate, to the achievement of National Vocational Qualifications (or relevant units) and, in Scotland, Scottish Vocational Qualifications.

An Investor in People takes action to train and develop individuals on recruitment and throughout their employment

i   Action should focus on the training needs of all new recruits and continually developing and improving the skills of existing employees.

ii All employees should be encouraged to contribute to identifying and meeting their own job-related development needs.

An Investor in People evaluates the investment in training and development to assess achievement and improve future effectiveness

i   The investment, the competence and commitment of employees, and the use made of skills learned should be reviewed at all levels against business goals and targets.

ii The effectiveness of training and development should be reviewed at the top level and lead to renewed commitment and target setting.

Figure 8.7 *Investors in People, principles of the national standard*

always a need to be sensitive to the unique characteristics of organisations, whose main goal remains delivering learning, when attempting to develop quality control systems for education. Learning is much more than a service which can be purchased in the market and compared to similar products. It is the result of a subtle set of interactions between the learner, the educational system and a range of other social agencies. In a very real sense the learner is partially responsible for the quality of his or her own learning and must therefore remain central to this evolving debate.

Further reading and references

Audit Commission/Office for Standards in Education (1993) *Unfinished Business: Full-time educational courses for 16–19-year olds*, London: Audit Commission/Ofsted.

Business and Technology Education Council (1992) *Centre-based validation – A handbook*, London: BTEC.

County of Avon (1989) *Evaluation – A process planner*, County of Avon Evaluation Strategies Report.

Department for Education (1993a) *Publication of information by FE Colleges*, Consultation Document, London: DFE.

Further Education Funding Council (1993a) *Assessing Achievement*, Circular 93/11, Coventry: FEFC.

Further Education Funding Council (1993b) *Funding Learning*, Coventry: FEFC.

Further Education Unit (1993) *Basis for Credit*, London: FEU.

Muller, D and Funnell, P (1991) *Delivering Quality in Vocational Education*, London: Kogan Page.

North West Quality Network (1992) *Quality Framework*, Liverpool: NWQN.

Glossary – An ABC of the Vocational Curriculum

The glossary provides a list and brief definitions of the main terms and acronyms used in the text. There is a page reference in almost every case.

ABC – A Basis for Credit – the title of a 1992 FEU project and associated publications concerned with developing a credit, accumulation and transfer framework for post-compulsory education (p88).

Access – the opportunities provided by the educational system to individuals for entry and progression beyond compulsory schooling (p104).

Accreditation – the process leading to the recognition of successful student achievement through the granting of an award (p109).

Academic appeals – student appeals against assessment decisions, based upon a formally approved academic appeals procedure (p69).

Andragogy – the theory of adult learning, which stresses the value of approaches which build upon the existing experience of the learner (p55).

APL – the accreditation of prior learning, a generic term which encompasses both the assessment and recognition of prior experiential learning (APEL) and the accreditation of prior certificated learning (APCL) (p96).

APLA – the accreditation of prior learning and achievement, an alternative to the acronym APL (p96).

Assessment – the process by which evidence of student learning and achievement is obtained and evaluated (p58).

BTEC – the Business and Technology Education Council (p12).

C&G – City and Guilds (p12).

Capability – an all-round human quality, the integration of knowledge, skills and competencies expressed in learner confidence (p74).

Case studies – detailed histories of real situations or incidents often used to relate and apply concepts and problem-solving skills to work contexts (p50).

Competence – the ability to perform tasks in real or simulated work roles (p18).

Core themes – cental and integrating themes which link the discrete elements of the vocational curriculum (p52).

Core skills – transferable life skills, often referred to as common skills, such as numeracy and communication, which form the foundation for the learner's success in work and education. Many vocational qualifications contain compulsory core skills units (p62).

Course – a curriculum, usually based upon a number of compulsory elements which are studied in a set sequence, over a set period of time (p41).

Course leader – the member of teaching staff responsible for co-ordinating teaching and assessment by the members of the team of staff delivering the elements of a course (p127).

Course committee – a formally constituted group consisting of tutors, students and employers who have responsibility for managing and developing the course. Meetings of the course committee usually have an agenda and are minuted (p48).

Course team – the group of teaching staff who work together to manage teaching and learning on the course (p127).

Course monitoring and review – the process of collecting and reviewing information to inform the evaluation of the success of the course in achieving its objectives for promoting student learning and achievement (p132).

CAT – credit accumulation and transfer, the process by which qualifications and past achievements are awarded educational credit so that students can transfer from one course or programme to another without undue loss of time (p80).

CPVE – certificate of pre-vocational education, an early foundation-level award aimed at preparing students for future occupational roles; it has been replaced by other awards, such as GNVQ foundation level (p120).

Credit – a measure of the volume and level of learning achieved on a module or discrete element of a course or programme (p84).

Criterion referencing – systems of assessment, such as NCVQ, which are based upon an explicit definition of the expected outcomes of assessment.

Curriculum design – the process of developing vocational courses and programmes akin to product development in commercial organisations (p26).

DOVE – diploma of vocational education, a foundation-level award offered by City and Guilds.

Education for Capability – an initiative sponsored by the Royal Society of Arts, concerned with promoting approaches which develop learner capability, such as the capacity for independent learning, in post-compulsory education (p64).

ENB – English National Board, the professional body responsible for validating nursing, midwife and some other health-related qualifications in England (p103).

Entry – the stage in a learner's career at which they enter a college or other educational institution, usually through enrolment and registration for an award (p43).

Exit – the stage in a learner's career when they leave a college or other educational institution, usually upon successful completion of a course (p43).

FEFC – Further Education Funding Council, the national body responsible for funding and external quality assessment in England (p140).

FEU – Further Education Unit, a national body concerned with the research into post-compulsory curriculum and the dissemination of good practice in further education.

Flexible learning – a generic term commonly used for three different aspects of the management of learning within an institution: a **flexible organisation** associated with open access to learning programmes and opportunities for assessment,

student-centred learning methods and **flexible learning structures** based upon modular delivery and credit accumulation and transfer (p45).

Formative assessment – assessments designed to give the student feedback about the success of their work, not necessarily used to contribute to formal assessment or grading (p46).

Franchising – situations in which one educational provider, for example a college or university, allows another institution to offer a course or learning programme for which it holds validation (p114).

General credit – credit or exemption offered to applicants in respect of past qualifications or achievements, usually in respect of the first stage or level of a course (p105).

GNVQ – general national vocational qualifications – a series of qualifications, primarily for full-time students in schools and colleges, designed to provide a comprehensive and coherent alternative to the GCE route (p18).

Guidance – the totality of institutional processes aimed at ensuring that the student is supported in his/her studies and chooses the correct programme and career route (p47).

HEFC – Higher Education Funding Council, the national body responsible for funding universities and higher education and for external quality assessment in this sector (p85).

HEQC – Higher Education Quality Council, the national body, funded by contributions from higher educational institutions, concerned with developing and furthering quality assurance across the new HE sector (p85).

Independent learning – a generic term used to describe approaches to learning which encourage the student to take responsibility for his/her learning often through the agreement of a written learning contract (p54).

Industry lead body – the national bodies, appointed by the National Council for Vocational Qualifications, consisting of representatives of employers and the professions that are responsible for defining the occupational standards for National Vocational Qualifications (p16).

Individualised learning – programmes designed to allow the individual learner to study at their own pace and time, often based upon open learning resources (p53).

Integration – the linking together of the discrete elements of a vocational programme, through such devices as cross-modular or integrated assignments (p52).

Internal validation – a quality-control procedure used by schools and colleges under which new or revised course proposals have to be approved internally, before external validation by the awarding body (p130).

Job competence – see definition of competence

Learning programme – modular and flexible structures of learning based upon open access and many exit points, permitting the learner a considerable degree of choice over what, when and how to study (p42).

Leaning outcomes – detailed statements of what the student is expected to achieve as a result of successfully completing a module or other component of a curriculum (p83).

Lifelong learning – a commitment to creating educational opportunities for individuals to learn and study, throughout their lives (p15).

MCI – Management Charter Initiative, the NCVQ lead body for management and supervisors (p163).

Module – a unit, usually free-standing, of learning and assessment (p81).

Moderator – an external assessor appointed by a national awarding body to monitor the standards achieved on a set of vocational courses (p33).

NCVQ – National Council for Vocational Qualifications, the national organisation set up in 1986 with the remit of rationalising vocational qualifications in the UK (p16).

NVQ – National Vocational Qualification, an award accredited by NCVQ as conforming to the standards set by an approved lead body (p18).

NETTS – National Education and Training Targets, a set of agreed objectives for increasing participation in the vocational education and training system and for raising standards (p15).

Norm referencing – assessment in which the standard ascribed to a candidate's performance is a function of that performance in relation to that of other comparable candidates (p74).

Occupational standards – levels of competence established and defined by an NCVQ industry lead body (p17).

Pedagogy – the art and science of teaching children, but more commonly associated with teacher-dominated approaches to learning (p55).

Performance criteria – the specific criteria associated with the assessment of NVQ and GNVQ units and elements (p61).

Pitman – one of the national awarding bodies (p12).

Portfolio of evidence – a collection of assignments, projects and other evidence to demonstrate successful achievement against learning outcomes and/or performance criteria (p49).

Programme leader – see course leader.

Programme team – see course team.

Pre-entry – the stage prior to enrolling or registering for a qualification (p102).

Professional Association – national organisations which represent the interests of their members (eg nurses, chartered secretaries) and also determine qualification routes related to entry to the profession (p13).

Quality assurance – the processes and procedures developed by organisations to ensure that quality of delivery is maintained (p126).

Quality control – implementation of system of quality assurance to check and verify that appropriate standards have been maintained (p126).

Referral – a situation in which a student marginally fails to achieve pass level in an assignment or end-of-course assessment (p68).

Resource-based learning – learning which is aided by physical resources, such as computers or printed or audio-visual material (p48).

HOW TO DESIGN A VOCATIONAL CURRICULUM

ROA – record of achievement, a file with evidence of students' achievements, including reports incorporating tutor and student comment, with a substantial element of self-evaluation and action-planning (p53).
RSA – Royal Society of Arts (p12).

Self-assessment – assessments in which the students makes an evaluation of their own performance (p62).
Simulation – a learning tool which is based upon a simple representation of reality to enable the learner to determine the critical variables in a complex situation (p50).
Student handbook – a guide written for students which provides a simple summary of the structure, content and assessment of a course or learning programme (p30).
Student-centred learning – approaches to learning designed to encourage students to take responsibility for the success of their own development (p54).
Summative assessment – the formal assessment process leading to grading and the determination of whether a student passes or fails a course (p59).

TEC – Training and Enterprise Council, referred to as LECs in Scotland or Local Enterprise Councils (p14).
TDLB – Training and Industry Lead Body, the NCVQ lead body responsible for setting standards for assessors and verifiers (p107).
TVEI – Training and Vocational Education Initiative (p120).

Unit of competence – a component of an NVQ award, which in turn is broken down into elements of competence (p60).

Validation – the process of gaining approval from an awarding body for a new or modified course or programme (p25).
Validity – the extent to which a course or programme satisfies its vocational purpose (p136).
Verification – the monitoring of the process of assessment to ensure that consistent standards are maintained, undertaken in the NVQ model by internal and external verifiers (p68).

Work-based assessment – the measurement of performance in the workplace, usually by a workplace assessor (p106).